The Anxiety Solution

A Revolutionary Guide to Calm, Clarity and Confidence

BY BELLA DODDS

WITH ROB VAN OVERBRUGGEN, PHD

Published by: ★LUMINARIES PUBLISHING
Text copyright © 2014 by Bella Dodds
Graphs copyright © 2014 by Bella Dodds
ISBN: 1502814471
ISBN-13: 978-1502814470

Disclaimer

The information in this book is not intended as medical advice; it is for informational purposes only. For questions about how to treat your illness, please consult your physician. The term self-healing/self-heal is referred to throughout this book. When used, it is solely referring to the body and mind's innate, scientifically proven, and biological ability to heal and repair itself. Self-healing is also used in reference to when an individual solves a problem, challenge, and/or stress in his/her life. The author is not stating that this book will heal you. The author is not a medical doctor. The author does not diagnosis, cure, or heal anyone. This book is not intended to diagnose, cure, or heal anyone. Please consult your doctor before reading this book. If you are taking medications, please consult with your doctor if you plan to change your dosage. Do not do so on your own. Changing your prescription without your doctor's guidance can be dangerous. This book is sold with the understanding that the publisher is not engaged to render any type of psychological or medical advice. Neither the publisher nor the author shall be liable for any physical, psychological, emotional, financial, or commercial damages, including but not limited to special incidental, consequential or other damages. Our views are the same: You are responsible for your own actions and results.

Dedication

To my mom and dad for their unconditional love and their support of my journey—a journey that has treaded off the safe and traditional path on more than one occasion. Thank you for letting me spread my wings. I am eternally grateful. I love you.

~ ~ ~

To my grandmother, who is one of the wisest, most inspiring women I know.

Free Twelve-Minute Guided Meditation to Relax Your Anxious Mind

This book is a guide to help you identify underlying stress patterns that are directly connected to your biological symptoms of anxiety; you will also learn a transformative method to help you resolve your anxiety and stress from the inside out.

While reading this book, and as a bonus, you may enjoy this relaxing, guided meditation to help you calm, soothe, and quiet your anxious mind. You can download it for free by going to:

www.belladodds.com/meditation

Table of Contents

Introduction

Before beginning this book, read this section first...

What if your anxiety is not a meaningless mistake? What if there isn't something wrong with you? What if your symptoms are a purposeful, biological response to specific, unresolved mental and emotional stress trapped in your body and mind?

This anxiety book is unlike any you will commonly find on the market today. Instead of just another list of techniques to help you cope with and manage your symptoms on a daily basis, this book will help you to discover *why you have anxiety in the first place* and *what you can do about it*.

We all know that anxiety is exhausting to manage on a daily basis, but I don't want to focus on your symptoms. I want to present something completely different.

My goal is to make this book as simple and straightforward as possible, to help you understand why you have anxiety and how you can resolve your symptoms from the inside out.

To do this I will explain three components of Integrative Health that are extremely important for you to understand and that make this book unique. These components will be segmented into the following three easy to read, comprehensive sections:

Section One: META-Health – Your Anxiety Is Not a Mistake

I will share important, up-to-date research with you on breakthroughs in health in the 21st century. In the past ten to fifteen years, technological advancements, such as high-speed internet and personal smart devices, etc., are changing the world—this is obvious. But what is less known are the technological advancements that have transformed our understanding of the human body and the way we look at health. This new information will be invaluable to learn not only for addressing your anxiety, but for any other health problem that may arise in your life or those of your loved ones.

In the first section, I will share several key models of META-Health, which are based upon empirical evidence built on over 30+ years of cases studies and brain CT scans, scientifically correlating the mind-body-emotion connection. META-Health collaborates with doctors, scientists, and health practitioners from around the world in an ongoing study to understand how the mind, body, emotions, and spirit come together in affecting health and disease; it explains how symptoms are the response to specific forms of stress and the biological purpose behind them. In essence, META-Health offers an accurate, scientific, and reproducible explanation of how specific mental and emotional stressors are directly linked to different diseases in the body and why. It enables a conscious shift away from fearing symptoms to understanding the underlying cause behind them. In this first section, you may well be exposed to information you have never heard before as we explore your anxiety from a META-Health perspective.

Section Two: How Unresolved Stress Creates Unconscious Beliefs That Intensify Your Anxiety

In the second section, we will investigate how your unresolved stress stays trapped in your body and mind, causing limiting beliefs and habitual stress patterns to form; these stress patterns then directly impact your physiology and trigger your anxiety. We will also look at how these repeating stress patterns create habitual, unconscious thoughts and behaviors that exacerbate your symptoms and keep you trapped in a vicious cycle. In addition, we will take an in-depth exploration into the nebulous components of your beliefs and how a simple *belief* can greatly affect your health in harmful ways by imprisoning you in endless worry. This section can be life changing for you if you allow yourself to reflect on it and really take it in.

Section Three: The Solution – Pain to Purpose and Transformational Exercises

In the last section, we will address the solution to your anxiety, and I will share with you a powerful, life-changing tool to resolve your past and present stress. Studies have shown that stress is linked to six leading causes of death—this is one of the driving forces for writing this book— and I want to share with you a revolutionary tool to help you resolve your stress more quickly and effectively. Stress is a part of life, and although you can't prevent yourself from experiencing challenges, you can learn to process life's stresses with much greater ease and self-mastery. In addition, you can't change your past, but you can *completely transcend your past* by evolving and growing stronger because of it. It is not what happens to you in life; it is how you perceive it, and most importantly, what you do with it. I want to teach you how to turn your greatest challenges into rungs on a ladder upon which you climb, and with each rung climbed, you'll be resolving your anxiety from the inside out. The chief aim within this book, and within the Integrative Health approach, is not to cover up or merely get rid of your symptoms, *but to use your anxiety in a powerful, life-changing way*. In the last several chapters, I will give you four powerful exercises to tie together everything you have learned within this book so that you will be able to apply these life-changing methodologies for yourself.

Know that I too have suffered with anxiety, so I am very clear on how you feel. I know how horrible it is to try to manage inner feelings of worry and unnecessary sensations of looming dread just going about your normal day. I know how hard you can be on yourself, how exhausting and draining it can be. I know how anxiety corrodes your health, internal dialogue, and confidence about yourself, your work, your interactions with others, your energy throughout the day, and your overall productivity in life. I can also tell you that I am profoundly grateful to no longer have to fight a daily battle with my adrenals pumping unnecessary levels of stress into my system. It is truly life changing to be able to get through my day feeling calm, thinking coherently, and acting in a steady and confident manner—even amidst a busy and stressful day.

But I didn't get there overnight. I used the principles in this book to overcome my anxiety and completely change my life...and now I want to share those secrets with you!

Now, one last thing before we get started. Know that I can share with you encyclopedias of information on how you can resolve your anxiety from the inside out, but unless you *believe* that this is possible and are committed to bringing your full Self to the process, it will be like trying to push a boulder up a mountain and having the boulder keep rolling back down just when you start to make progress. **You are your most powerful asset to your health by far.** When you understand how important you are in the self-healing equation, your journey from symptoms to wellness will shift tremendously from a path that moves away from fear, anger, and being overpowered by your circumstance to one that moves toward self-accountability, curiosity, commitment, intimate participation, and growth on *all* levels of who you are. When you fully appreciate how important *you* are in the equation, your empowered position fuels your conscious knowing that if your body had the ability to create symptoms of dis-ease, then you and your body together have the power to self-heal. Your role in restoring your own health is at the top of the list. Not your doctor, not your therapist, not your nutritionist, not your coach, but *you*. And like most things in life that have powerful truths based upon simple equations, your effectiveness depends upon what you *believe* about it. Understand that no matter what I share with you or what brilliant health professional you work with, if deep down you believe someone else has to fix you or you believe that your symptoms are hopeless because you have been diagnosed, and the facts are the facts—and if you believe you will have to suffer with them for the rest of your life—then please know that your 24-hour, 7-days-a-week, month-after-month, year-after-year, moment-upon-moment *belief* will inevitably cause you to prove yourself right.

This is how powerful you are.

On the other hand, if you believe that there is something you can do to correct your anxiety, you are committed and determined, you take full responsibility for your health, you are ready to address the core areas causing stress in your life, and deep down, you believe that your body has innate self-healing capabilities, then everything you do, every healing resource you choose to undertake will be infused and fueled by the power of your knowing. And this knowing will completely transform how you perceive your health, how you choose to treat your symptoms, and what your journey will offer you through a deep and rewarding process on a path from symptoms to health.

This is how powerful you are!

The 21st century paradigm of health, disease, anxiety, and self-healing is what I will share with you in this book, and if you have the courage and willingness to go deep into the heart of what is connected to the anxiety in your life, your self-healing journey can offer you one of the most meaningful, heartfelt, and purposeful experiences of your life.

"Healing is a matter of time, but it is also a matter of opportunity."

~ Hippocrates

... I'll one up Hippocrates and add that healing is a matter of *great* opportunity.

Now let's get started!

SECTION ONE

1

21st Century Anxiety – A Life Changing Approach

You have begun a journey that can add depth, meaning, and beauty to your life in ways you might not yet be able to fathom. However, to help you resolve your anxiety from the inside out, and awaken to the hidden opportunity within your symptoms and within this book, we'll first need to build a solid platform from which you can grow. You can imagine the Integrative Health approach as being similar to when you first meet someone who changes your life.

When you first meet this person, the tone might be slightly formal as you get to learn the basics about each other—the first section of this book will be like that. It will be the framework that you can build upon and move forward with.

When you start to get to know this person better, you become more authentic, heartfelt, and open with each other—the second section will be more about who you are as a person and how your thoughts and emotions impact your health and well-being in all areas of your life.

Then, when you experience the life-changing moment where you deeply resonate with this person; when you transcend space and time and feel like you have known him/her all your life—the third section will be more of this quality, offering flashes of insight and opportunities to connect with yourself on a Soul level in ways that are life-changing.

In essence, to self-correct your anxiety, we will start with your biology, and then move deeper into your mind and emotions, then deeper still into the inspiring, powerful realm of your spirit. As I said, Integrative Health encompasses and addresses all levels of who you are, which is why it has the opportunity to be a fulfilling, life-changing process.

So please bear with me as I get practical in this first section and share with you the basics of what you need to know to understand your anxiety from a logical, scientific perspective.

17th Century Health vs. 21st Century Health

In our society, we are taught from a young age that disease, to a large extent, is a weakness and breakdown of the body, while simultaneously being led to minimize our body's innate ability to heal and repair itself. Yet, this perspective is not helping us to be healthier, but rather is leading us to be disempowered and to live at the mercy of our symptoms. If we want to achieve a higher level of *health*, an important first step will be to evolve to a higher understanding of the human body. For centuries, the predominant consensus has been that disease is a mistake of the body with no meaning behind it and therefore must be numbed, medicated, cut out, or poisoned. Additionally, disease has been studied primarily at the physical level without investigating an individual's life circumstances and well-being on all levels to try to understand *why* the body is responding with certain symptoms.

To offer you invaluable information and breakthroughs in the field of anxiety and health, we will be looking at your anxiety from a 21st century perspective, which addresses your symptoms by taking into account your health on a biological, mental, emotional, and spiritual level. And the interconnection of your mind-body-spirit leads us to the field of META-Health.

As a META-Health Coach, I am trained in the scientific understanding of how mental and emotional stress creates physical symptoms and disease in the body. META-Health, as described above, offers an accurate, scientific, and reproducible explanation of how specific mental and emotional stresses are directly linked to different diseases in the body and why, enabling a conscious shift away from fearing symptoms to understanding the underlying stress behind them.

But how does META-Health achieve this?

META-Health works through the understanding that the body has evolved for millions of years, and as such, has a highly evolved biological program to survive the many demands of the environment. In the 1980s, a medical doctor in Germany named Dr. Ryke Geerd Hamer, discovered that when the body experienced a highly shocking and stressful event, its psychological and physiological impact could actually be seen via brain CT scans. The CT scans revealed that stress ring patterns formed in particular areas of the brain depending on how an individual *perceived* the stress; additionally, the area of the brain that processed that particular type of shock was not an accident. Each region in the brain is connected to a specific organ and is equipped to elicit a meaningful organ response to meet the demand of a particular form of stress. Yet, when the mental and emotional stress component is left out of the equation and is not investigated, then the organ response will be viewed as a mistake, symptoms will appear as meaningless, and the cause will remain unknown.

We will explore this in great detail shortly, but for now, I will quickly state that chronic symptoms, such as anxiety, are often due to unconscious fears and unresolved stress trapped in your body and mind, which is continually triggered by day-to-day stress. When you understand this mind-body connection, you can resolve your stress, thereby supporting your body to heal itself.

Why have the mind, body, and spirit been separated in the study of health and science?

During the 17th century, René Descartes, the philosopher and founding father of modern medicine, was forced to make an agreement with the church in order to study the body. Human cadavers were illegal to dissect under church law, so Descartes made an agreement that the body was distinctly separate from the mind, emotions, and Soul and that those aspects of human existence were under the exclusive jurisdiction of the church. The church agreed to designate the body to medicine, which from that moment on imposed a limiting paradigm that would affect Western medicine and science in the study of human health and disease for centuries to come.

At first, mastering the understanding of human physiology worked brilliantly and has, without question, **contributed to an _invaluable_ understanding of health and disease and has saved the lives of millions of people**; however, as decades go by, wide gaps are beginning to appear that are now impeding progress. The big problem with this approach is that we are not just human _bodies_, we are human _beings_. There is a monumental difference between the two. Which begs the question, how can a human being be fully understood and healed if it is divided into separate fields that are *not separate at all*?

The undertone in Western medicine is that anything beyond tangible biology is not taken seriously or is not real science; however, we only need to look at history to get the complete picture as to where this strict black-and-white thinking originated from, because if you really stop for a minute *and think about it*, separating the mind from the body is actually *incredibly illogical*. For instance, if you are anxious, you do not experience this as a mental concept floating next to your body—you *feel* anxiety flooding every cell of your body!

So how can you separate the mind from the body? The truth is you can't. We have just been conditioned to think this way. If you have ever been under a great deal of stress, you've undoubtedly noticed how it impacted your digestive system, sleeping patterns, immune system, etc. We have been taught to take an antacid, a sleeping pill, etc., but although they can successfully mask the symptom, neither gets to the source of the problem. Mental and emotional stress will impact *all* levels of who you are simultaneously. When you understand this, it makes logical sense why anxiety and any other health problems you might have cannot fully be resolved by treating the physical level alone. As we incorporate consciousness into biology, a totally new ballgame emerges, and it changes the traditional way we perceive and treat symptoms. This is the next evolutionary leap that we must take because we are not just human zombie's walking around *without* consciousness—we are mentally, emotionally, and spiritually experiencing life through our bodies as human beings. Therefore, if we experience a very stressful event, this mental and emotional stress will impact us on all levels; and if our stress is left unresolved and untreated, it will continue to affect our physiology, leading to symptoms over time.

To empower you with a scientific understanding of how stress creates anxiety and other diseases in your body, I will share with you five models that are the foundation of META-Health. **Understanding these models will be *essential* to working with your anxiety in an integrative approach, as well as creating the foundation on which we build within this book. Bear with me for the next several pages...once you understand the basics of these models, we will then use this information and apply it specifically to your anxiety in the next chapter.**

META-Health Models

Model 1: Your Human Body is Highly Intelligent

A core foundation within META-Health is that your human body is *highly* intelligent; however, I don't want you to just take my word for it. Let's take a brief look to get a clearer sense of exactly what I mean.

First, I'd like you to reflect on a time, perhaps a holiday gathering, where you had a group of relatives squished together into a house for a day. Think back...did any drama arise? How harmonious was that loving family get-together of four to ten people for five hours? Key word here is *harmonious*. Or what about the functionality of your country's government—is there a consistent flow of working together in an organized, highly effective, cooperative fashion, or is there a bottleneck of gridlock, disharmony, and corruption? Now try and keep these two examples fresh in mind as we explore an intelligence that organizes 50 trillion cells within your human body.

For instance:

- How does your body transform wavelengths of light into your ability to see color, shapes, and spatial dimensions?
- How are you able to think, feel, and speak?
- How does your body digest food, breathe oxygen, and circulate life-giving nutrients to each one of your 50 trillion cells?
- How do you turn sound waves into cognitive communication? If someone yells at you to run, how do you digest the sound, translate it into meaning, and then switch into a sympathetic state and run like crazy?
- How does your body heal a broken bone or deep wound?
- How does your body reproduce and create the next generation of life?
- Do parents have to consciously oversee and direct every stage of cellular growth and development of their baby, or does the intelligence and miracle of life take care of this?
- And what organizes the coherent function of your brain made up of 200 billion cells linked together by hundreds of trillions of synapses?

"In a human, there are more than 125 trillion synapses just in the cerebral cortex alone. That's roughly equal to the number of stars in 1,500 Milky Way galaxies"

~ Dr. Steven Smith

If we admit that we do not control these amazing human functions, this raises the question:

Why do we not trust the profound intelligence that gives us life and seek to work in harmony with it…but rather try to overpower and outsmart it?

Neil deGrasse Tyson once famously said, "We are all made of stardust." This poetic reflection comes from the astonishing realization that our bodies are made up of the atomic elements that were once forged within the furnace of distant stars, and these ancient stars scattered their enriched, life-giving contents across the universe through stellar nucleosynthesis. These supernova explosions billions of years ago formed gas clouds that eventually collapsed, birthing new stars and planets rich with the chemical elements of oxygen, carbon, hydrogen, nitrogen, calcium, and phosphorus, which are now the building blocks within our bodies. The common origin of our most distant relatives is not from this planet, but from ancient stars, and these chemical elements *somehow* coherently organized together to give us *the miracle of life*.

> *"Our common origin is in the center of a star and the molecules in my body are traceable to phenomenon in the cosmos. It is not that we are in the universe, but in fact given the chemistry of it all, the nuclear physics of it all, not only are we in the universe, **the universe is in us**."*

~ Neil deGrasse Tyson

I say 'somehow' because the most brilliant minds in our history both past and present do not yet know what organizational force causes these chemical elements to come together to create highly complex cells, which build into different tissues, organs, and organ systems that make up highly evolved human beings. If you took all the ingredients of a heart cell and shook them up in a petri dish, the elements would not magically fuse together to create a functioning, intelligent, living cell. One thing is clear—the sole difference between 'living tissue' and 'dead tissue' is organization. Dead tissue lacks an organizational *force of intelligent energy* to unify matter into coherent function.

Understanding that your body has an innate wisdom that is highly intelligent is at the *core* of the new paradigm of 21st century health. For your human body, made up of approximately 50 trillion individual cells and 500 trillion microbes, in looking at these numbers it is actually quite logical, rather than whimsical, to speculate that there must be an intelligent organizational force that is able to coordinate these trillions of cells and microbes to cooperate in a common goal of survival. In an attempt to help you grasp the sheer volume of this inconceivable number, here is a picture of the Milky Way galaxy, which is estimated to boast a mere 200 billion stars.

In truth, you are your own micro-universe with a magnificent orchestration of trillions of microscopic events taking place inside you to such an unfathomable level that it is next to impossible to fully comprehend the complexity of everything that transpires to keep you alive for just one minute. The function in one cell alone (said to be made up of 100 trillion atoms), is extraordinary to understand even if you grasp just 1% of its life-giving function. Perhaps because we have an abundance of cells, it is easy to minimize their value, but the truth is that each cell in your body is an *individual organism* that—just like you—breathes, eats, digests, eliminates waste, communicates, processes complex information, reproduces, and senses its environment through a highly complex and evolved cell membrane. And yes, all of this and much more takes place within each and every microscopic cell within our bodies.

Now try to conceptualize 50 trillion cells joining together in synchronization, forming into specific tissues that build into different organs that then evolve into complex life-giving organ systems: cardiovascular, nervous, endocrine, skeletal, muscular, cranial-sacral, integumentary, digestive, excretory, reproductive, meridian, and respiratory that all cooperatively work together to give you life! Your body allows you the ability to perceive, breath, see, touch, smell, taste, and live, love, do, and be who you uniquely are in the world. The truth is that your body is one of the greatest gifts you will ever be given! We are conditioned in our society to fault our bodies for everything that goes wrong or to devalue ourselves if we do not match the current trend of beauty. Consequently, we have a tendency to minimize our body's extraordinary intelligence and to buy medications and beauty products to fill emotional voids or to 'fix' ourselves, driven by unconscious beliefs that 'there is something wrong with me,' and 'I am not enough.' Yet, through this self-limiting mindset, we are drastically discarding the **innate beauty and power of life**

within us. The truth is that trillions of microscopic events are taking place at every moment, within every breath to keep you alive.

From this brief summary, is it safe to intuitively trust that there must be some intelligent force that organizes *MATTER* into *LIFE*? And if there is, how intelligent might this ancient, star-enriched photonic energy be to orchestrate and organize the 50 trillion cells within your body?

Furthermore, what possibilities might exist if you were to learn how to work *with* this innate intelligence to self-heal your anxiety, rather than work against it?

> *"We come nearest to the great when we are great in humility."*
>
> ~ Rabindranath Tagore

Model 2: 85-95% of all Disease is linked to Stress

It has been estimated that 85% or more of all disease is linked to stress. Dr. Mercola recently said, "It is well-accepted even with the traditional medical community that there is a strong connection between emotions and health. Even the conservative CDC, the Center of Disease Control, stated there is an emotional connection in about 85% of all physical illnesses."

We can define stress as strain put on the body due to a number of contributing factors: mental, emotional, dietary, social, physical exertion, or environmental toxins. Interestingly, the unifying component within all of these stress-induced aspects is how an individual *perceives* the stressful experience. For instance, dietary intake often has a high emotional and mental component, as does experiencing the effects of environmental poisons. The mental and emotional element is infused within *every* experience of life—conscious or unconscious—and is called Synchronous Unity Awareness in META-Health. This means that stress is experienced on all levels of your organism simultaneously; therefore, your anxiety must be resolved on all levels of who you are, not just on a biochemical level.

In addition, different forms of stress will affect your body uniquely. For example, the body must respond biologically to the stress of starvation, the force of being attacked from another human being, being isolated and abandoned, or losing one's job or loved one. **One physiological response does not sufficiently match all of the variables within human life.** Challenges are wide and complex, and the type of stress will determine the type of strain the body must absorb and biologically respond to in order to meet the demand. Other factors include how long an exposure is and the level of its severity. Severe stress over prolonged periods of time will have a greater impact on the body and cause more challenging symptoms, which often take longer for the body to heal and recover from...unless you take a proactive approach and support the body to self-heal on all levels: mental, emotional, physical, and spiritual. The body's self-healing process can be speeded up dramatically.

In relation to your anxiety, we will be looking specifically at what stress and organs are connected to your anxiety; however, please do not skip ahead, as this information all ties together and is explained in a comprehensive, sequential order.

Side Note: Your Body is a Healing Machine

Your body is masterful at healing itself. That is what it was designed to do, is fully capable of doing, and does every night while you are sleeping. However, your human body is a biological organism and requires certain elements to be able to maintain good health. Take a plant, for instance. If a plant was placed in a dimly lit room, with stale old soil, and sporadic watering, this organism would soon suffer and become sickly; however, if you took the same plant and put it into a brightly lit room, gave it fresh soil filled with abundant minerals and nutrients, and you watered it regularly, this same sickly plant could totally revive, heal, and repair itself. Your human body is no different. It has certain requirements for health as well, and as we progress into this book, you will learn that when your body is under a great deal of stress, it goes into survival mode and delegates its energy resources into protecting you and keeping you alive. Therefore, if you are carrying high levels of unresolved stress, this could be seen as the equivalent of being in a dark room—eventually your body, as a biological organism, would become compromised and symptoms would appear.

Model 3: There are Two Phases of Disease

This META-Health model is based on the research of Dr. Ryke Geerd Hamer, MD, who discovered that the human body responds to mental and emotional stress in a Two-Phase Disease Process: First Stress Phase and Second Regeneration Phase. **This is incredibly valuable information to know and understand for your own health.** The majority of the population believes that when they become sick, the body is weak, or that their symptoms are a random breakdown and error of the body. From the new 21st century paradigm on health, we recognize that mental and emotional stress has been scientifically proven to have a direct impact on the physical body, initiating a specific two-phase process of disease.

Two Phases of Disease

Symptoms and illness are often triggered by a highly stressful event that was unexpected, dramatic, and has no immediate solution. A complete progression from the beginning of a disease through the healing is described as a disease process. The typical symptoms of an illness such as anxiety, muscle pain, headache, flu, ulcers, insomnia, or more serious health issues are not the illnesses per se, but a partial aspect of a comprehensive disease/healing program in the body. The intensity, energy, and length of the Stress Phase is approximately equal to the intensity and length of the Restoration Phase. **(That is, unless you assist the body to self-heal by resolving the underlying emotional stress, as well as providing the body with healthy foods, adequate rest, etc. You can speed up the Restoration Phase dramatically!)**

There are nine specific points within the two phases of disease, which are seen in the graph below. I will explain each one of these points briefly.

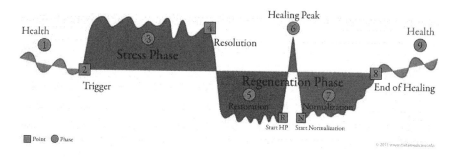

The Nine Points of the Two Phases of Disease

1. **Health** - The body is in a healthy balance of normal day and night rhythms.
2. **Stressful Trigger** - A UDIN moment occurs: An **U**nexpected, Highly **D**ramatic, **I**solating event with **N**o immediate solution to resolve the problem.
3. **Sympathetic Stress** - The body is in a heightened sympathetic state of mental and emotional stress and is biologically responding to solve and adapt to the conflict that has occurred. The body is not able to switch fully into its nightly rhythm to rest and repair and is in overdrive trying to cope with the conflict. (Common symptoms: sleeplessness, poor appetite, obsessive mental and emotional stewing, stomach ulcers, obvious change in personality)
4. **Conflict Resolution** - The event that triggered the conflict has been resolved and the body is no longer adapting to meet the demands of that stress. The reversal is usually triggered by the stress no longer being present or the problem having been solved. The body can now move into the second phase to restore, heal, recover, and repair.
5. **Regeneration Phase** - The body is in a parasympathetic state of fatigue, rest, recovery, and repair. It goes into deep healing and recovery from the buildup of strain placed upon it. Obsessive mental and emotional stressors lose their charge. In this phase, many different types of undesirable symptoms like the flu, headaches, diarrhea, aches, and pains can occur, even though the actual disease started weeks, months, or years before. **(This creates a gap in the obvious link between the mind-body connection and the stressful event that**

triggered the ensuing symptoms. META-Health makes the link between cause and effect, while seeking to understand why the body biologically responds the way it does to meet the demands of stress placed upon it.)

6. **Healing Peak** - This is the point where the body flips from a Restoration Phase into Normalization. Imagine driving and you need to go in reverse. First you need to stop the car, shift, and then press the gas again. To stop and shift gears is the healing peak as your body shifts to normalization

7. **Normalization** - The body is still in recovery, though on the mend. Symptoms are less severe and beginning toward normalization.

8. **End of Healing** - The healing phase is complete from the body taking on and surviving the stress.

9. **Return to Health** – The symptoms are resolved and the body returns to normal night and day rhythms and energy levels.

You can see that if you experience a highly stressful event your body will be affected by that stress and biologically respond *to help you get through it*; however, **it must go through a healing process afterward**. It may not be convenient, but wear and tear is wear and tear, and your body must heal, recover, and repair! The good news is, if you address the underlying mental and emotional stress, you can speed up your body's recovery time tremendously.

If you are under a great deal of stress, it is important to not isolate yourself, or try to absorb all of the stress on your own for weeks or longer. Seek outside counsel with friends or family, a coach, a therapist, an acupuncturist, etc. The essential point is not to ignore your stress or your symptoms—focus on solving the problem. For instance, if we used a stress scale, from one to ten, with ten being the most extreme, and you reduced your stress from a ten down to a manageable one to three, you will be able to see and think more clearly, be more calm, make rational, wise decisions, eat better, and be able to sleep. Can you sense the difference this will have on your body and your health? Doing this would also be practicing preventative medicine by resolving your stress before it created *inconvenient* symptoms later on.

Model 4: Stress is Measurable on Brain CT Scans

For this short section on brain CT scans, I want to introduce to you my fellow colleague from Rotterdam, Netherlands, Dr. Rob van Overbruggen, PhD. The CT scan aspect of META-Health is quite fascinating, and I thought it would be valuable to you to have him share his knowledge and expertise on the subject, as well as provide visual images so that you can have a clearer sense of what we are talking about. In the next chapter, we will talk about brain CT scans specifically connected to your anxiety and the corresponding organs.

Excerpt written by Rob van Overbruggen, PhD.:

My first introduction to this material was back in 1995. At that time, I was fascinated by the use of external machines that could check what trapped emotions or stressful issues were still living within a client's mind.

Brain CT scans are used by mainstream medicine to take a look inside the body to see what structural changes there are. This can be used to diagnose a bone fracture or other diseases inside the body. Another use for CT scans is to see if there are ruptured blood vessels in the brain. Basically, they make a photo of the structure inside a human body, whereby they take many sliced images, and each picture of a CT scan is actually a sliced image of your body.

In META-Health, we use the CT-scan information to understand what emotional stressful issues a person experienced in his/her life. These emotional issues can have four different stages:

- Fully resolved
- Active
- Resolving
- Chronic

When the emotion is fully resolved, there is no trapped energy in the brain anymore so you do not have to work on it. This would be like if you lost a teddy bear when you were a child, but it does not bother you at all anymore.

The other option is that the emotion and process is still active. The CT scan shows clear markings to indicate that the emotion and disease process is in the active Stress Phase, which means that an individual still has a lot of trouble around this issue. If you have anxiety, this means you are in an active Stress Phase. Recurring obsessive thinking, stressful feelings, no appetite, etc. are first Stress Phase symptoms, which can be clearly seen in a brain CT scan. For example, imagine that a child was hit by a car, and he is in the hospital, and doctors fear for his life. During this period of stress, the mother of this child would clearly show the Stress Phase markings if a brain CT scan were taken. In this case, the stress is clearly active in this person; however, if the stress is never fully resolved, it can also become a chronic repeating pattern of stress that lasts for years. (Therapeutically, this is highly important, as a person would need to resolve his/her specific stress as soon as possible.)

Here is a recreated image of the rings within an active first Stress Phase conflict as seen in a CT scan:

Here is a magnified image of an actual first Stress Phase conflict from a CT scan:

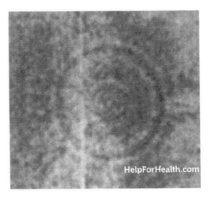

The third type of ring pattern is the Regeneration Phase when the body is repairing the situation and moving back toward normality (meaning that the stressful emotion is resolved and does not bother you, but at the same time the body still needs to repair). In the case above with the mother and child in the hospital, the markings in the brain will move towards resolution when the child is back into safety and the mother feels that everything is okay. Imagine extra cells being created in the Stress Phase to deal with the situation, but when the body is no longer in that stress, what does the body do with the excess of cells? Now the extra cells need to be decomposed, the body switches into the Regeneration Phase, and this phase can be observed through a CT scan.

Here is a recreated image of the rings within the Regeneration Phase as seen in a CT scan (notice they are more blurry and less defined rings):

The chronic state of the brain marking shows that the emotion is not resolved, but occasionally (or often) comes back. For example, if you are afraid of dogs and never overcome this fear, then you will be triggered by seeing a dog. You will have stress for a few minutes (active). Then when the dog is gone, you are relaxed (resolving), but a few weeks later you go over the entire process again. Therapeutically, this means that there is still work to do to fully resolve the issue.

How easily these markings can be found depends upon the intensity of the trauma and the duration of the stress. A very short trauma cannot be seen. An intense trauma that lasts for years will always be visible to the skilled practitioner.

For example, when a person perceives a very intense stress, the body-mind needs to react to solve the situation. In order to do this, the stress impacts the brain to actually make sure the organs start to react. So for example, when you need more blood to your heart to be stronger, then the impact point of the EMAP (Evolutionary Meaningful Adaptation Program) will be on location to direct the coronary artery's lining to become thinner. Because the lining will be thinner, the volume of blood going there will be larger and the person can run faster or fight harder.

The markings of the brain are actually the energetic holdings of the emotion that is stored in that brain location, and this stressful energy alerts the organs what to do. You will see how this applies to your anxiety in the next chapter.

Interestingly, the energy of the emotion affects the brain structures like throwing a pebble in the water. The rings that appear in the water are energetic waves of the water molecules. The same phenomenon is present in the brain. When the energetic information is perceived, the waves become visible until the emotion is fully released. On a CT, you can see the rings on multiple slices. Looking at the pebble again, the rings not only appear on the surface of the water, but they also appear beneath the surface. This happens with a mental and emotional stressful energetic impact point too. It is a three-dimensional impact point that shows the markings on different slices just as energetic waves of the water molecules. The same phenomenon is present in the brain. When the energetic information is perceived, the waves become visible until the emotion is fully released and resolved by that individual.

*Dr. van Overbruggen is author of *Healing Psyche - Patterns in Psychological Cancer Treatment*, a book that scientifically proves that working with emotions and beliefs changes the course of cancer. http://www.healingpsyche.com

If you are interested in learning more about cancer and the underlying stress with cancer, his book is available on Amazon.

Model 5: Symptoms are a Biological, Meaningful Responses to Stress

This is our last model! Thank you for your patience in learning this important information!

As shown in Model 1, your human body is intelligent; therefore, its response to stress is also intelligent. This means that your anxiety is not a weakness of your body, rather a meaningful, evolutionary response. META-Health looks at how specific organs respond differently to stress, some initiating a cellular increase (to amplify organ function), and others initiating a cellular decrease (to reduce organ function).

In the next chapter, we will explore what organs are specifically connected to your anxiety, what mental and emotional stress is correlated with these organs, and how your anxiety is not a mistake, breakdown, or weakness of your body, but rather it is a biological, intelligent, evolutionary response.

Great work getting through this section! Now that you have a greater understanding of META-Health, we can delve deeper into applying what you have learned and link it specifically to your anxiety.

2

Your Anxiety is Not a Mistake

In this chapter, I want to teach you how to investigate and discover *specifically* what unresolved stress is connected to your symptoms. I want to help you get to the source, to the root of what is triggering your anxiety—because this is where your power and freedom lie. I believe Integrative Health is simple and complex at the same time. It is simple once you *get its essence*, and then a domino effect can occur, spurring your intuition to innately understand your body and health in a much more holistic and logical manner.

The empowering perspective I want to offer you in this book is that you have anxiety for a reason. It is not a random mistake of your body, it is not something that you have to feel powerless against, and no, you do not have to be stuck managing your anxiety for the rest of your life. It also doesn't have to take years of therapy to clear your symptoms, especially when you know exactly what triggers and stress patterns require your attention. I am not saying it will be easy and effortless to change your conditioned patterns, but anxiety is not fixed—it is an adaptive, biological, unconscious pattern that can be resolved.

First of all, your anxiety is not as connected to your present life circumstances as you may think. Your current stress can *easily camouflage* itself as something to worry about; however, the *root*, the real root to your anxiety has a great deal more to do with *unresolved stress* and *adaptive survival responses from your past*. This unresolved stress accumulated over time and built up tremendous pressure in your body. A good analogy is likening this pressure to the pressure behind a dam. A reservoir, like your body, has a max capacity stress load that it can successfully manage without problems arising. However, if the max capacity of a dam is breached, the town below would have a big problem on its hands; likewise, if your body's homeostatic capacity has been breached by too much stress—you will have a problem on your hands too in the form of symptoms. Getting to the root stress and releasing this pressure is the key to helping you self-correct your anxiety and resolve your symptoms from the inside out.

And I am sure you have had enough of coping with your anxiety and you are sick of trying to suppress your symptoms on a regular basis, otherwise you probably wouldn't be reading this book! If you are **ready** to get to the heart of the matter, then here are three powerful questions to investigate and ask yourself. (I would like to say, please be gentle and mindful with yourself while you are reading these questions. Don't go intensely into memories on your own; just skim the surface with conscious acknowledgment. If you start to feel too triggered, then simply stop, skip the questions, and move onto the case studies. You can still glean great insight and clarity on the source of your anxiety.)

Three Questions to Ask Yourself

Scan your childhood and adult history and explore:

1. Did you experience a dramatic event that was highly stressful and/or unexpected? For example:

- Did your parents get divorced?
- Did you move unexpectedly?
- Did you have to change schools growing up?
- Were you bullied?
- Did you witness intense fighting?
- Did you unexpectedly lose your job?
- Were you ever in a car accident?
- Did a loved one die unexpectedly?
- Did a loved one or parent die from a chronic illness like cancer?
- Did you find out your partner was cheating on you?
- Did you have an unplanned pregnancy?
- Were you sexually abused or molested?
- Were you verbally abused?
- Were you physically abused?
- Were you raped?

Any of these stressful events can create a habitual, unconscious pattern of anxious thoughts causing you to be on high alert (even when there is no cause to be worried). Additionally, you can feel a deep sense of responsibility coupled with anxiety as you try to make sure everything will be okay and that everyone, including you, will be safe.

2. Did you grow up in a household where there was alcoholism, drug abuse, or a volatile parent?

- Did you grow up in an unpredictable environment not knowing if one day you would feel safe and the next day not?
- Did your parents fight a lot—cut-the-air-with-a-knife, passive-aggressive manner, and/or in an explosive fashion?
- Did you ever have to step in to protect a parent or sibling?
- Were you constantly on edge around an intoxicated parent?
- Did you grow up with a mentally ill parent who was verbally and/or physically abusive?
- Did you grow up with a parent who was very depressed?
- Did you grow up with a loved one who had a chronic or terminal illness?
- Do you now get anxious worrying about others?
- Do you now put others' well-being above your own?
- Is it easier for you to focus on helping others than it is to focus on yourself?

Years of being in an unpredictable environment can massively affect your biology and conditioned thought patterns, causing you to constantly be on guard and anxious, not knowing what threat or drama may happen next. Growing up around addiction often causes children to develop hypersensitive perceptions, and to be highly tuned in to their environment as a way of protecting themselves in an unpredictable and sometimes volatile upbringing. This fear and hypersensitivity to the environment can last well into adulthood as an unconscious anxious pattern, and foster a highly sensitive nervous system that tunes into subtle cues from someone else's mood, body language, tone, and/or temperament. You can be so tuned into your environment and trying to meet other people's needs that you neglect your own well-being, and this can cause you to feel spaced out and overwhelmed as you try to process too much emotional information...your emotions as well as everyone else's in the room.

3. Did you grow up with a perfectionist or highly critical parent?

- Did you have a highly critical parent that you were anxious to be around or feared disappointing?
- Did you feel pressure to get exceptional grades or have a perfect weight and/or outer appearance?
- Did you feel tremendous pressure to excel as an athlete, performing artist, etc.?
- Did you feel pressure from a parent to put on a show of perfection for your school or town when in reality this was far from the truth?
- Do you now find yourself trying to manage five million things by yourself?
- Do you have extremely high self-expectation to do everything the best that is absolutely possible...in other words, do you feel like you have to do *everything perfectly*?

Growing up with a perfectionist, highly critical parent, or being sensitive to social stereotypes of perfection can lead an individual to be highly self-critical and anxious as they are constantly striving to do everything perfectly, pretty much *every minute of the day*. This impossible self-expectation adds up to a lot of pressure on a daily basis.

Let's look at two case studies to really clarify this:

Case Study #1

Will's Anxiety

Will is a 30-year-old single man who suffers from extreme anxiety and poor sleep. He feels he has to manage his anxiety every day, which can reach overwhelming peaks of eight to nine on the one to ten scale (ten being most anxious).

Will's History

Will is the oldest of three kids. He has a brother one year younger and a sister three years his junior. During his childhood, he often lived on edge. His whole family did. He grew up with a father who was an alcoholic and whose behavior was highly unpredictable. Whenever he came home, Will wasn't sure if he would have to brace against an angry, volatile father or a more docile energy. His father had a very frightening temper at times. It seemed that Will would get yelled at on a regular basis, as well as witness his mom, younger brother, and sister getting yelled at, which he hated but felt powerless to do anything about. Living in the house was unbearable at times, with numerous incidents that caused him to feel great fear. **One instance in particular stands out in his memory.** At age nine, he witnessed his father irately yelling at his mom and throwing food and furniture around the house. He hated it but felt like there was nothing he could do to truly protect her. Sometimes he hated being at home. Some days were great, but he never really knew when the good days were going to be and when the bad days were going to be, and because of this unpredictability, Will, under the surface, lived in a constant state of unease. He feared doing anything wrong that might get him into trouble and force him to have to deal with his father's unpredictable temper.

We will discuss Limiting Beliefs in the next chapter, but for now, know that Unconscious Limiting Beliefs are created during stressful experiences. For years, Will was under stress, which unconsciously caused him to believe: *I am not allowed to relax. I have to be hypervigilant or bad things will happen. I am not safe. I have to do something to make sure everything is okay. I can't mess up or I will be attacked and get in trouble. Life is hard. Life is unfair. I am stuck. Feeling safe and good won't last for long.*

Case Study #2

Grace's Anxiety

Grace is a 38-year-old mom of two children and she experiences high levels of anxiety every day. She is a very hard worker and a self-proclaimed perfectionist. She can feel extreme anxiety just getting herself and her kids ready for the day, going to the store, or doing basic tasks at work, etc. She feels she doesn't have any control over her extreme worry, and when her anxiety takes over, she has trouble thinking clearly and accomplishing tasks with ease.

Grace's History

Grace grew up in a middle-class family, and she had one brother who was two years older. Grace felt a tremendous amount of pressure from her parents to do well, especially in school where there was always a very high expectation on her to excel. Her parents told her that doing well was essential in life, so Grace pushed herself hard to get straight A's because getting anything less was not an option. At age fourteen, her family moved unexpectedly, and Grace felt totally overwhelmed leaving the safety of her friends and starting school in the middle of the year where she didn't know anyone. After her family moved, she began to feel even more on edge around her mom, who started to be overbearing and strict. Her mom didn't like anything out of place and there was more than one occasion when she got frighteningly livid. Sometimes it could be about the house not being clean, or other times she would flare up if Grace did not score a high mark on an exam. So Grace tried not to upset her mom. She kept the house tidy, did well in all of her courses, and looked the part of a high-achiever by being meticulous in her appearance. Her parents' high expectation for her *did* push Grace to excel, but she also grew increasingly critical of herself and always felt a steady grip of pressure towards elitism and to be perfect in everything she did.

Grace developed the following Unconscious Limiting Beliefs: *I have to be perfect. I have to do everything perfectly. I am not good enough. Nothing I do is ever good enough. I am not loved for who I am. They don't see me. If I can make them happy then they will love me. I have to earn love by doing everything perfectly.*

Next we will look at track patterns and how an accumulation of a repeating stress can lead to developing anxiety.

Track Patterns and Anxiety

For starters, what exactly is a track pattern?

A track pattern is a sensitive, reactionary button that unleashes intense emotions inside you when it gets triggered by someone or something. Your anxiety has an unconscious track pattern connected to it, for example. It is a sensitive button that takes you out of your rational thinking mind, where you might otherwise respond with more poise, and instead it triggers your sensitive, unresolved past stress. When this happens, you will be flooded with anxiety and irrational thoughts.

A track pattern can also be seen as a train track because it creates a habitual, one-way response to how you **perceive and react to stress**. For instance, let's say four people with the same role in a company got laid off. They all experienced the same stressful event, but each one perceived losing their job differently. The first person reacted with deep feelings of rejection, thinking he was a huge failure in life and fell into a depression for six months. The next person responded with optimism. For a while she had felt like her job wasn't challenging her at all and getting let go was a blessing in disguise and exactly what she needed to go after what she really wanted in life. The third person obsessed about everything she must have done wrong, coupled by tremendous fear of now living in uncertainty and feeling terrified of having to put herself back on the job market. The fourth person responded thinking that it was the company's loss—what a bunch of idiots they were to let him go! He now felt totally invigorated and inspired to kick some ass and show the world what he was made of.

As we can see, each person reacted differently and told themselves a story about what happened, and *gave the event a unique meaning*. This is a key understanding to have: it is not what happens to you—it is how you perceive what happens to you and the meaning you give to it.

Why do you respond to stress the way you do? What meaning do you give to your stress?

Know that the default story you tell yourself feels very real and intense for you. Why? Because it is your track pattern with a lifelong story to share with you if you take the time to stop, get curious, and investigate. To discover what story you are telling yourself, first you want to investigate how you react when something stressful happens, big or small.

To give you an idea of what I mean, here's an example:

First, let's say sometimes you feel anxious because you don't feel completely safe and secure, and even if everything appears to be okay, you still feel like something bad could happen and you are on edge. But why do you feel this way? Where does this anxious feeling come from?

The next step is to feel your anxiety and then ask yourself:

When was the first time I remember feeling this way? (Follow your anxiety back to its source of origin.)

For example, perhaps the first time you remember experiencing a highly stressful event (say witnessing an intense argument or getting severely punished), it was very scary for you. Reflecting back on it you can sense that the same *looming dread* that you experience today on a regular basis, is actually the *same* feeling of looming dread you felt when you were younger.

If the anxious sensation feels *familiar*, this is a good sign that you have found your track pattern—same feeling, just different circumstances. The reason for the similarity in feeling, regardless of the different circumstances, is because when you experienced a highly stressful event for the first time, your body and consciousness recorded the event; then the next time a challenging event occurred, your senses might have warped that experience slightly by **seeing it through the lens of how the *previous event had affected you*.**

Another way of looking at it is that a track pattern creates a colored lens that slightly warps what you see, and this colored lens greatly affects how you *think* and how you *perceive* what happens to you. Over time, as you accrue more stressful experiences, *how* you perceive stressful events begins to denote a *similar theme* in your perception, while strengthening your jaded lens that affects the *meaning* you give to what happens to you. This lens could be a feeling associated with, 'I am not safe. They are going to hurt me,' and whenever you feel unsafe (whether there is a direct cause or not—an unconscious thought can trigger your anxiety), your button gets triggered, causing a rush of anxiety to flood through your body, quickly followed by a knee-jerk reaction of anxiety to protect yourself and be on high alert. And as more stressful experiences accumulate, your track pattern will grow stronger and more sensitive over the years, greatly influencing your mental, emotional, physical, and spiritual health.

For example, we can look at our case study with Grace, who grew up with a critical parent who reprimanded and belittled her whenever she messed up. These stressful events could, without a doubt, have created a track pattern in her conscious and unconscious mind as an *acute inner wound* and vulnerability to being criticized. Her track pattern could create problems later on in her life if left unresolved, as an acute trigger and overreaction to whenever she felt she was being criticized—*even if the other person was not intending to demean her at all*. But after years of being criticized, it makes it *extremely* difficult for Grace not to take criticism personally. Why? Because all of her unresolved emotions from being belittled as a child rush to the surface, flooding her body with heightened, unresolved emotions, completely taking her over. Even if Grace *logically* knows someone is not trying to be hurtful, her unresolved stress makes it nearly impossible for her *not* to feel anything else *but* hurt, and because of this, she has challenges in her personal relationship, as well as an intense need to have everything done exactly how she wants it. Sometimes, if her anxiety becomes too much for Grace, she cuts people out of her life, walks away from business opportunities, or doesn't take effective action in her career due to a gripping inner fear of messing up and being exposed to more criticism. Grace's unresolved track pattern also fosters negative self-talk, deeply corroding her confidence and sense of well-being. To compensate for all of this stress, she sometimes self-medicates through overeating, overspending, over-exercising, watching too much television, and/or drinking too much wine. This repetitive stress-react-self-medicating cycle never resolves Grace's core issue, and eventually leads to chronic and acute anxiety. Grace's current life challenges trigger her greatly, but to resolve this problem, Grace needs to address the root of where it began in the first place. For as a 38-year-old adult, being run by her **track pattern and unconscious 8-year-old fears** is unquestionably holding her back massively in life.

From an Integrative Health perspective, you can see that your body is actually communicating to you through its symptoms that you have an outdated, limiting stress pattern holding you back. Your body is one of your greatest teachers because it cannot lie. Its symptoms are an accurate map guiding you to exactly what you need to resolve in your life. The good news is that within your stress is an untapped opportunity to turn your greatest adversity into your greatest strength. I will go into this in great detail in Chapter 6: Pain to Purpose, but before we jump ahead, there is more you still need to learn about your anxiety from a META-Health perspective.

For instance, why does Grace's track pattern lead to anxiety?

In the beginning of this chapter, I mentioned that your body, like a dam, has a max capacity threshold for pressure and stress; and if a dam's capacity is breached, the town below will have a big problem on its hands. The same is true for your body. A track pattern leads to accruing too much stress that will eventually breach your body's homeostatic threshold, forcing your physiology to meet the demand with a heightened organ response, which you will then experience as chronic anxiety symptoms.

If you are a visual learner, here is a figure to help you understand how stressful events can create a sensitive track pattern that then leads to anxiety symptoms overtime:

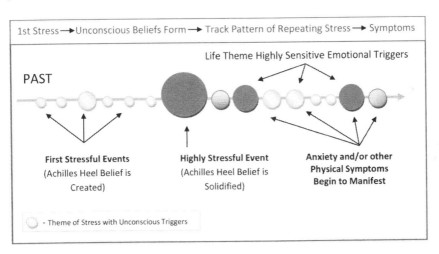

Another visual way to understand how accumulated stress leads to symptoms in the body is through the figure below. Can you see the upper and lower homeostatic limits? The fluctuations within these normal limits are your night and day rhythms. During the day, you are under stress, versus the evening when you are in rest and recover mode; however, when a highly stressful event triggers your sensitive track pattern, you might breach the homeostatic limits and symptoms will begin to appear as your body must respond to meet the demands of the perceived stress.

Stress Levels Breach Homeostatic Limits

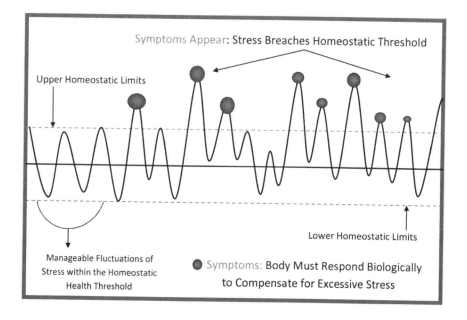

Your Anxiety Track Pattern Was Created in Your Youth

To self-heal your anxiety, the essential understanding to have is that your track pattern is a *conditioned lens* that was created by your developing consciousness when you were young. Your symptoms of anxiety are alerting you to not only clear your unresolved stress, but also to clear your childhood lens and consciously replace it with an adult perspective. I think we can agree that two-, five-, seven-, and fifteen-year-olds have a certain way of *reacting* to life that are indicative of their age, and their perception about the facts are not always 100% accurate. Your track pattern was created in your youth, and it created a reactive lens that affected your belief about yourself, life, and other people. These perceptions are outdated and counterproductive to the many responsibilities you have to manage in your adult life, and while they may have helped you survive while you were younger, they can now be relentlessly holding you back as an adult.

I have worked with clients in their 70s who can get deeply emotional about what happened when they were five years old, just as easily as someone in their 20s, 30s, and 50s can. Why? Because emotions and memories are powerful! Powerful enough that 70+ years later a stressful event can still be alive inside a repressed consciousness, and can still be **powerfully** affecting the lenses in which individuals look through, how they see the world, how they feel about themselves, and how they react to life. As an adult you might intellectualize the past by saying you are 'over it now' or you have 'forgiven your parents' and anything else that might have happened, but this is often only *intellectual*. Your body and unconscious still have to manage trapped, unresolved stress that you don't want to look at—so even though the past is in the past, it actually *isn't*. Unresolved stress is still alive in your present, stored as energetic charges of tension in your body and mind. What I find again and again with my clients is that these unresolved, deeply ingrained stress patterns create unconscious Achilles Heel *present-day* stress triggers. These triggers continue to accumulate more stress until too much builds up, breaching the threshold of what your body and psyche can manage—leading to chronic and/or acute symptoms of anxiety.

I want to point out that none of this is a weakness. I have yet to work with one person who does not have a track pattern running—it is actually a purposeful evolutionary survival aspect within our developing consciousness that was designed to keep us safe; however, life is not as black and white anymore. Our flight, fight, and freeze response does not need to be activated 50 times a day. We don't have to associate a stressful environment as life or death situations anymore, like being taken out by a lion for instance. Our bodies evolved to record highly stressful environmental cues to protect us and alert us to similar dangerous environments in the future as a way of survival, but in the modern world (more often than not) this is no longer an advantage, but a hindrance. We are still evolving and developing as a species, and it appears the next level of development may not be to grow another set of opposable thumbs to survive, but rather to develop our higher conscious faculties for navigating and processing past and present stress.

Now that we have looked at what stress might be connected to your anxiety, let's look at your symptoms from a new perspective...a purposeful one.

21st Century Anxiety: A Purposeful Biological Response

In the first chapter, I mentioned that if you experience a highly stressful event, the impact of this event can actually be seen on a brain CT scan. Interestingly, it is not a random occurrence which area of the brain absorbs the stress, as specific areas in the brain correspond to organs that then biologically respond in a purposeful, intelligent way to meet the demand or threat.

In the case of anxiety, there are at least two active conflict shocks in the prefrontal cortex, one on the left hemisphere and one on the right hemisphere. The prefrontal cortex is the area of your brain located behind your forehead; if you ever get headaches in this area it can be due to an active brain-relay Anxiety Constellation.

The term 'Constellation' is used in META-Health when there are two or more conflicts that land on the left and right hemispheres of the brain. For example, when an individual goes through a stressful experience and a shock is absorbed by the cerebral cortex, it will land on either the right or left hemisphere; however, when a second conflict shock occurs and is absorbed in the cortex, this shock will land on the opposite hemisphere and the individual will go into what is called a Constellation. This means that the body cannot handle the stress sufficiently through only a biological organ response and must make an essential change in the psyche of an individual to help him/her survive the conflict.

The change in psyche becomes either a more manic or a more depressive energy. A more manic energy has a decrease in estrogen, giving an individual more drive to fight or take action to overcome a challenge or threat. A more passive energy is a decrease in testosterone, causing an individual to be more adaptive to circumstances by being more peace-oriented, inert, non-confrontational, and possibly depressed. Because META-Health Constellations are an in-depth topic, and in an effort not to not bombard you with excessive information that is not pertinent to understanding anxiety, I will keep this as simple as possible.

Just know that in the case of anxiety, there are at least two active conflicts that land on the left and right side of your brain located in your prefrontal cortex. Below is a CT scan of an Anxiety Constellation provided by Dr. van Overbruggen. Look closely and you will be able to see the light rings of trapped emotional energy. (If you or a loved one suffers from depression or manic-depression, and you would like to understand more about constellations, please sign up for my newsletter at www.belladodds.com and mention your interest. I will be hosting a training that covers this topic in depth.)

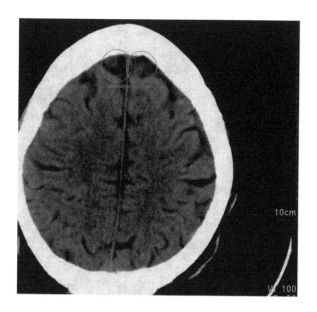

In the slide above, you can see the light ring patterns circled in red. On the right hemisphere of the pre-frontal cortex is the organ-brain relay Pharyngeal Arches, and on the left, the Thyroid Excretory Ducts. What is somewhat mysterious about these two organs is that they are active and form during embryological development but do not have a classical organ function after development as compared to the obvious organ functions in the stomach, colon, and lungs. More research is being done to understand these two organs in the Anxiety Constellation; however, we do know the essential components of the mental and emotional shocks that trigger these two organ-brain relays. Below, I will share the underlying stress that activates anxiety within the Pharyngeal Arches and Thyroid Excretory Ducts.

If you have anxiety, you most likely would have these two ring patterns show up in a CT scan due to the two conflicts listed below:

1. Frontal Fear - Pharyngeal Arches

Conflict Shocks:

- Fear of attack or being attacked
- Fear of future attack or problem

Commonly Caused By:

- Watching parents fight
- Seeing an angry authoritative figure yelling at you
- Fear of being criticized by an overly critical parent
- Seeing a car coming right at you in an accident
- Being verbally or physically attacked
- Seeing someone else who is being verbally or physically attacked
- Being in an environment where someone (perhaps a parent) is in constant stress—fearing lack of money, security, instability, etc.
- Unexpected event of someone dying
- Fear of a loved one who has a life-threatening illness dying
- Fear of being verbally, physically, or sexually abused

When you experience these types of stress, you may have corresponding emotions and thoughts of:

- "I am afraid."

- "Something bad is going to happen."
- "Something is wrong."
- "They might get mad."
- "I am going to get in trouble."
- "I don't know what is going to happen."
- "I am not safe."
- "What is going to happen when they die?"

Client Case Study of a Frontal Fear Shock

An example from one of my clients who experienced a Frontal Fear:

At age 21, she received a phone call from her friend, a police officer, who was calling to tell her that her mother was physically attacking her sister. He asked her over the phone, "Do you want to get there first, or do you want us to go?" She was twenty minutes away in a car and remembers experiencing extreme anxiety of not knowing what she would find when she arrived.

Unconscious Stress Trigger: Auditory Trigger of phone ringing and cop verbally telling her a stressful, unexpected event and being afraid of what she would find. Her stress tested over a ten on one to ten scale. Before she worked with me, she had been triggered by phones ringing, which set off an inner dread and horrible worry that she would receive bad news.

2. Powerlessness - Thyroid Excretory Ducts

Conflict Shock:

- Feeling powerless

Commonly Caused By:

- Feeling powerless, helpless, and completely overwhelmed by a stressful situation
- Not in control; wanting to be in control but being completely powerless
- Feeling at the mercy of a catastrophe or crisis
- Feeling vulnerable
- Feeling overpowered by someone
- Feeling unfit, ineffectual, helpless, impotent, or weak
- Feeling powerless in life or a life circumstance

Corresponding Emotions and Thoughts Can Be:

- "There is nothing I can do."
- "It's hopeless."
- "I can't handle this - it's too much."
- "What can I do?"
- "I can't do anything."
- "I am overwhelmed."
- "I hate this, but I am stuck and can't get away."

Client Case Study of a Powerless Conflict Shock

Shortly after the event mentioned above with her sister and mother, this same client experienced a Powerless Conflict.

During this period, she went back to work, but when she walked into her office, she totally broke down in tears. She felt completely powerless and unable to handle the demands of her job in addition to the family crisis.

Second Stress Trigger: Stress of feeling powerless with her responsibilities of work and dealing with her family. Visual Powerless Trigger occurred at work, being unable to cope with life and the demands of work. Stress tested eight to nine on one to ten scale. Post event—seeing a messy room or feeling overwhelmed by the pressure of dealing with the daily demands of the world triggers her anxiety and overwhelm.

Integrative Coaching Included: Releasing life-stress patterns associated with the Frontal Fear of fearing the worst was going to happen and being attacked, as well as resolving the Powerless Conflict of feeling unable to cope with the daily demands of her life. The origin of these two patterns actually began when she was 5 to 7 years old due to repeated stressful instances with her alcoholic mother, but eventually manifested as extreme anxiety at age 21 from the conflicts mentioned above.

Biological Purpose of Anxiety

As mentioned earlier, constellations cause mania and depression when you experience two or more highly stressful events; however, unlike other constellations, the Anxiety Constellation does not cause mania or depression (unless another brain relay is active and we will discuss that more shortly.) The two conflicts of **Frontal Fear** and **Powerlessness** absorbed within the pre-frontal cortex land on the most evolved area of the brain, which has to do with higher thinking, problem solving, and future planning. It has been theorized (and further research is being done) that the trapped energy of these conflicts in this area of the brain causes an amplification of the prefrontal cortex's function of problem solving and future planning/preparing. The trapped stress held within the pre-frontal cortex triggers amplified, rapid thinking to solve problems projected into the future.

For example, many individuals with anxiety are trapped in the psychological pattern of incessant worry, problem-solving, future planning, organization, and fast-paced thinking. They are in a state of great angst just going about their normal affairs because tasks are accompanied by an amplified intensity and hypervigilance of everything that needs to be done, causing an individual's mind to race in a panic. Many individuals with anxiety create large to-do lists that overwhelm them with disproportionate and unnecessary levels of urgency, coupled by a heightened sense of responsibility. Additionally, anxiety often causes individuals to be run by fear of not messing anything up and needing to do everything perfectly, highly aware of the ramifications if they make an error.

Anxiety can also be fueled by feeling there is a problem that needs to be solved *immediately* to prevent chaos or something bad happening, which creates a habitual and **unconscious inner need to be in control**. The feeling of not being in control and not having one's security and needs met can amplify anxiety considerably; hence, the pre-frontal cortex functions of future planning through problem-solving goes into overdrive. Needing to be in control and being a perfectionist (and/or a workaholic) are two very common themes I see over and over again with my clients.

Why is this common for people who have anxiety?

Imagine if an individual grew up with chaos, uncertainty, or unsafe feelings; can you see how this could easily create an unconscious need and desire to be in control and get everything in place so that his/her environment feels peaceful, safe, pleasant, and secure? Children who didn't have security and stability when they were younger often want to feel safe and secure to a high degree as an adult.

In addition to this, my theory is that trapped stress in this area of the brain also leads to developing heightened intuition, helping individuals to sense things before they happen, and/or tune in to subtle alterations within the environment by seeing and feeling more than what others might be able pick up on. Perhaps the prefrontal cortex is linked to our intuitive sixth sense and our ability to tune in to the future before things happen, as a way to be more prepared for unexpected chaos. It is possible that the biological response in this area of the brain is more of an energetic response by developing the intuitive sixth sense, unlike the classical organ functions of seeing, hearing, touching, digesting, etc. Many of my clients who have anxiety have heightened levels of intuition and sensitivity to their environment. I too share this experience—it is as though I can feel this area of my brain becoming more active, trying to tune in to what is going to happen next. When my anxiety was acute, it felt overwhelming, almost like it was short-circuiting, causing me to have headaches or feel dizzy and out of my body; however, now that I don't have anxiety anymore, it feels active but clearer.

Okay, now let's look at if you have anxiety, but also struggle with feelings of fatigue, and/or depression. If this is the case, you might also have an additional conflict shock running.

Anxiety and Fatigue

If you have anxiety and you also experience a dramatic drop in energy levels after being high strung and anxious for hours, your physiological symptoms suggest that you have another brain relay active. If you are feeling overwhelmed with **Powerlessness** and **Frontal Fear**, this can trigger a third conflict shock that can hit your Adrenal Medulla. The Adrenal Medulla can elicit a drop in energy levels or feelings of depression after the conflict has been resolved. For example, if you are working throughout the day in a somewhat high-level, anxious pace on tasks run by rapid, anxious thoughts, but then you switch out of being hyperalert in to a very low energy, fatigue, or depressive state thinking, "What is the point? It's too much," you might have the Adrenal Medulla brain-organ relay active as well.

3. Intolerable Stress - Adrenal Medulla

Conflict Shock/Stress:

- Overload of unbearable or intolerable stress

Corresponding Emotions and Thoughts Can Be:

- "I can't take anymore."
- "I am at the end of my rope."
- "It's too much."
- "I am at my wit's end."

- "I can't handle all of this!"
- "I am so overwhelmed."

Organ Biological Response: Increased release of neurotransmitter production—norepinephrine, dopamine, and epinephrine—triggering the sympathetic fight or flight response to have increased energy to deal with the stress.

In the Stress Phase, the Adrenal Medulla will increase organ function, thereby producing more stress hormones and causing you to feel anxiety. The loss of energy or feelings of depression can occur when you are no longer being triggered by a mental or environmental trigger, causing the Adrenal Medulla to switch into the second phase, thus decreasing organ function. With a decrease in organ function, **your energy levels will plummet**. If the stress pattern is left unresolved, this active-brain relay can lead to overtaxing of the adrenal glands and lead to adrenal fatigue.

Anxiety Summary: Evolutionary Adaptive Response

The human body has evolved for millions of years to biologically adapt to its environment for survival. If you grew up in a stressful environment with tension, criticism, high expectations, unpredictability, fighting, getting bullied at school, alcoholism, drug addiction, and/or threat of safety over a period of years, and/or you experienced shocking, unexpected events like your parents getting divorced, a parent or loved one dying, moving schools, moving to a new town, or country, I hope it is now clear how these circumstances can and do directly lead to developing anxiety. Additionally, these repetitive unresolved emotions and thoughts develop neural networks in your brain that strengthen over time. These neural links affect the way you perceive your environment and how you respond. You literally can get stuck in an anxious way of thinking, causing you to experience the same story over and over again—possibly with new characters, but with the same hurtful theme. These patterns are heavily anchored and backed by the strength of emotional charges built up over time that are not easily undone unless you address the core stress that caused them to exist in the first place. Even if you are free from a stressful environment now, your thoughts, actions, and behaviors are deeply ingrained in an unconscious track pattern of the past that triggers your anxiety.

The Good News

There is good news in this, I promise you! The good news is that the human brain is not static as once thought; it changes conditioned neural networks in your brain when you release and clear out your unresolved stress and limiting beliefs. Neural links that were formed from a child's perception can be unlinked, and new, healthier, mature links and perceptions can be made. As Yoda once said, "You must unlearn what you have learned." This is certainly true and equally possible.

One half of the solution in working with your symptoms is to know you have anxiety for a reason. It is not a random mistake of your body, it is not something that you have to feel powerless against, and no, you do not have to be stuck managing your anxiety for the rest of your life. It also doesn't have to take years of therapy to make these changes, especially when you know exactly what triggers and stress patterns require your attention. I am not saying it will be easy and effortless to change your conditioned patterns, but anxiety, like the human brain, is not static—it is an adaptive, biological, unconscious pattern that can be resolved.

Beliefs + Solution

I wrote this book to empower you with an in-depth understanding of anxiety so that you can see a logical way to overcome it and to correct it from the inside out. Now that you understand the potential source of your anxiety, it's time to learn how to undo these long-standing, ingrained patterns, which I will cover in the next two sections.

First, we'll look at your limiting beliefs:

This is such an important topic. *Such an important topic!* To shift your anxiety pattern, you *must* address the stress-inducing limiting beliefs that are locking this pattern in place. In fact, META-Health practitioners and others in the field of Integrative Health are discovering that limiting beliefs play a direct role in creating disease in the body. This may sound like a bold statement—after all, beliefs aren't *real* and they aren't a *physical* toxin you ingest—but in the next chapter, we will delve deeper into truly understanding beliefs and why they are linked again and again to symptoms in the body, as well as learn how they are massively holding you back in life. It is critical to master this chapter and recognize the harmful effects of your limiting beliefs, grasp the logic in how they got created, understand the importance of rising above your wounded childhood emotions (no matter how true they feel in the present), and to rise to an empowered adult position by understanding the necessity of upgrading outdated beliefs to healthy, life-supporting ones.

Second, we'll focus on the solution:

Stress is a part of life. We can't avoid it. But we can learn how to use it in incredibly beneficial, life-changing ways. People who have anxiety have a propensity to want to solve problems quickly and impatiently jump ahead, but please make sure you read the belief section first. If you want to utilize the transformative methodology and exercises I am going to share with you, you will *need* to know how important it is to upgrade your limiting beliefs or you will be working against yourself unnecessarily. And who the heck wants to do that?!

With that said, let's jump into it and explore what beliefs really are, why they are so powerful, and how they are playing a monumental role in keeping you stuck in a limiting, anxiety-inducing reality.

SECTION TWO

3

The Power of Beliefs – 'Be Life'

Welcome to the beliefs section! I love this topic. Beliefs are profoundly powerful, but unless you understand their power and consciously work with them, you will inevitably be negatively run by them. Limiting beliefs are directly connected to amplifying your anxiety. This may seem like a bizarre statement, so to better grasp this concept, we first need to understand exactly what beliefs are in order to be aware of how they can lead to health problems.

The word 'belief' is used quite casually in the English language, rarely invoking significant cause for examination. Yet, skimming over and barely recognizing what 'belief' means and what *it actually points to* is equivalent to looking at a pot of gold and assuming it is just fool's gold with little to no value; when in actuality, if you stopped and took a closer look, you'd realize you have in your hands a pot of pure gold worth 'mucho friggin' dinero.'

This chapter is important. I want you to really take it in and reflect on how it relates to you personally on a very deep level. I hope by the end of this section you will have a better understanding of why beliefs are so powerful and how you can use them in a conscious and positive way to help self-correct your anxiety and change your life for the better. Also keep in mind, you may already have an idea about the concept of beliefs, but I want you to *know* their influence *beyond a shadow of a doubt.*

> *"It ain't what you don't know that gets you into trouble. It's what you know for sure that just ain't so."*

> ~ Mark Twain

I am trying to self-heal my anxiety. Why do I need to know about beliefs?

Your beliefs are the set of rules that you live by, whether you are aware of it or not.

You created these rules long before you were ever aware of what you were doing, and these rules are based on what you have experienced, what you have consciously and unconsciously taken on from your environment, what assumptions you formed about life under challenging circumstance, and what you have been taught by your parents, school system, society, and/or religion. All of these outer influences directly influenced your perception of the way the world works, how you think about yourself, how you respond to life, and how you think and act—essentially, your beliefs are the set of rules that you live by and that govern your life.

However, your beliefs are not absolute; they are not a 100% fact, no matter how much your mind thinks they are.

I'll give you an example.

It is fair to say our global *belief of time* unites the majority of humanity as human civilization has agreed that time moves forward in a clockwise rotation. When you look at a clock and watch the hands progress clockwise, it feels right, doesn't it? It makes logical sense to see time moving *forward*. It would be odd to look at time moving 'forward' in a backwards, counterclockwise rotation. However, even though we were taught from a young age to look at time progressing clockwise, on a galactic level, we are taught something completely opposite to this. If you observe the Earth's North Pole from space, you would see our Earth orbiting around the sun *counterclockwise*, which means that if we look at our earth from our classical top/bottom, Northern/Southern Hemisphere perspective, we are cruising through space, traveling 67,000 mph around the sun, progressing in time going...*backwards*. However, if you look at the Earth from upside down in space, or perhaps more accurately described look down at the Earth's South Pole, you would observe our planet rotating around the sun, progressing forward in time in a *clockwise rotation*.

Did we perhaps get it wrong? What if the map of the world *actually* looks like this:

Is it odd after looking at the world map thousands of times right side up to suddenly see it upside down? Do you *like* what you see? Would you be cool if it suddenly changed to this tomorrow? How would it affect your engrained *belief* system?

The pictures of Earth taken by astronauts who are floating around without gravity and without a definite up or down reference say, "Earthlings, look at our beautiful planet from outer space. Isn't our Earth amazing! This is what we look like! Wow!" And the unbelievably cool pictures we get back are not of Africa, Antarctica, and Australia kickin' it at the top of the globe with mostly ocean surrounding the Northern Hemisphere. No, we predominantly see pictures solidifying *our conditioned belief* of how we have been *taught* to perceive the Earth.

Yet, logically, if we think of time as spinning forward in a clockwise rotation, then shouldn't our macro version of one year in time match our micro version of one day in time? If we wanted this to make congruent, logical sense moving forward, wouldn't it mean we'd either have to turn our image of the world upside down, or change the way we perceive time? Do you think we should start teaching the next generation to view the world map this way? Should we change our global language and instead of saying, 'We're going down under,' say, 'we're going up over to Australia?' Should North Americans become South Americans?

Can you see how one simple flip in conscious perspective can have massive implications?

Our belief systems are challenged when we look at things from a new vantage point or have new evidence that makes us question their validity. Northern societies may have come up with the traditional map of the world based on their location and reference point, but that doesn't mean their passed down point of view was right.

So which is right? Our sense of how time moves forward, or that our northern countries are really the ones on top? Is there even a *right* way of perceiving time and the world?

The fact is we don't even know how big the universe is, let alone which way is up and which way is down. Our modern concept of the universe is still a great mystery to us. Who knows? Maybe there is not one clear way to look at our world—and perhaps time does not *just* move forward in a clockwise orbit. If you look at a clock on the wall it moves clockwise, but the same clock looked upon through the wall from the back ticks counterclockwise. So which is it? The truth is, it is your position and perspective that determines what you see...and this holds true for looking at life on a grand scale as well as pulling back and looking at yourself. **It is not what happens to you; it is how you *perceive* what happens to you that will determine what you see and the meaning you give it.**

Now let's bring this back specifically to you. You too have made assumptions about life and what you believe are true and not true about reality, and these beliefs lie hidden within the core of all your life experiences. Your beliefs are foundational reference points for how you create, perceive, and experience your map of the world. They are your internal power (or limiting power); they are what you believe deep down to be true about yourself and what you believe to be true about 'reality.' Your beliefs determine how you feel and think about your self-worth, and thereby, directly influence and permeate all your thoughts, emotions, actions, fears, limitations, habits, perceptions, reactions, dreams, relationships, finances, and health. You *believe* 'this is how life is' and 'this is who I am,' and therefore, you will believe certain things are possible and not possible for you.

Your beliefs formed in childhood have a funny (or rather not so funny) way of imprisoning you well into adult life. For instance, let's say you grew up getting good grades in school and had parents who reinforced your confidence. Years later if your boss asked you to give a presentation at work, you might automatically rise to the challenge and not be too concerned with what people think about you, but rather be more energized to share your knowledge. Believing yourself to be highly intelligent, you'll hold a steady posture as you speak with fluent confidence. If, on the other hand, you grew up struggling in school, felt you weren't as smart as everyone else, and worried a lot about what others thought of you, giving a presentation at work you might feel self-conscious, and your posture might shrink as you stumble over your explanation. Although these two people can have equivalent knowledge, capability, and intelligence, one individual *believes* in him/herself while the other does not. One person feels confident; the other feels anxious and is gripped by the **limiting belief**—*I am not smart enough*—even if this is not at all true.

Yet, beliefs are as implied—they are *just beliefs!* This is so important to keep in mind. They are not concrete facts forever set in stone. We as individuals and as a society often mistake many of our beliefs to be facts, and therefore, limit and burden ourselves in copious ways, such as when we judged individuals' worth and intelligence by the color of their skin, when it was believed that women were too emotional to vote, or when men thought they were the superior gender. Oh, my, the humor! ☺ It is a bit difficult to fathom, but remarkably, it was less than 100 years ago that women were given the right to vote in the United States after a Federal Law for Women's Suffrage was passed in 1920. France passed their law in 1944, and Switzerland's smallest canton, Appenzell Innerrhoden, finally passed women's Suffrage in 1991. 1991?!

Beliefs can take time to change, but once they are changed, it is hard to even contemplate going back to such a limiting reality. **Please know that changing your limiting beliefs is equally possible. When you upgrade your beliefs, it will feel completely foreign to you to go back to your old, self-limiting way of viewing yourself or the world.** For when you adamantly decide to upgrade an inner child belief, you simply won't identify with your old paradigm anymore, just as millions of women around the world can no longer identify with the idea of not having the right to vote.

You Unknowingly Distort, Delete, Exaggerate, and Minimize 'Reality' to Prove Yourself Right

You continuously strengthen your certainty around your beliefs by 'adapting' your perception of reality to match your beliefs about it. Remember, it is not what happens to you; it is how you *perceive* what happens to you. For example, if you really believe life is hard and unfair, your conscious and unconscious mind will maximize and exaggerate any time a situation occurs where your belief is being proved right; and equally you will delete, distort, and minimize events that don't match your belief. For instance, imagine going to the supermarket when you are overcome by a sweet tooth. First you go to the massive freezer aisle and stare down the hundreds of kinds of ice cream. Next you go to the bakery section and drool over the countless pies, cookies, cakes, muffins, and other goodies. Do you think in that moment you'd be thinking how bloody unfair your life was? Well, maybe you would be if you were on a restricted diet and you were deathly afraid of eating processed foods, or if you were on a budget and couldn't afford what was right in front of you. Then you might maximize your feeling and affirm, "Life is not fair. This sucks." On the other hand, if you were in the habit of eating whatever you craved, had the money to afford whatever you wanted, and were not on a restricted diet of any kind, you might feel grateful to have so many options. Please keep it fresh in mind that it is not what happens to you...it is how you *perceive* what happens to you and, most importantly, the *meaning* you give to it. (No, this will not be the last time I say this. It is a crucial understanding to really get if you want to self-heal your stress and change your life.)

"Something that I thought I was seeing with my eyes is in fact grasped solely by the faculty of judgment, which is in my mind."

~ René Descartes

Another prevalent example is you can believe that one of your parents is mean, therefore your memories are mostly of him/her being cruel because your belief inadvertently maximized memories of when they were cruel, while equally minimizing or deleting memories entirely of when your parent was neutral or even being kind. Many of my clients who grew up with a challenging parent are trapped in a polarized childhood perception of only remembering their parent as cruel, and they often struggle to recount any clear memory of when their parent was supportive. To be clear, I am not saying that abuse does not happen. It happens to a horrible degree, all of the time, but having worked with people for years, I can tell you that being stuck in a polarized wound does not support physical health as an adult and often creates unwanted challenges in relationships. We'll get more in depth on why this is at a later point, but for now just know that black-and-white beliefs tend to have a high emotional charge that runs you mentally and emotionally, causing you to create blame, guilt, and stress in your life.

Now let's go deeper and make this discussion more grounded by looking at beliefs from a scientific perspective.

Scientific Theories and Beliefs

Scientific theories, like religious beliefs, greatly shape our model of the world that become dogmatic 'truths' over time, but they are not always correct and, when proven wrong, have massive ripple effects that change the world. Some examples include when we collectively used to *believe* that the world was flat; when it was heresy to say that the earth was not the center of the universe; when we feared disease was due to evil spirits or bad karma; when scientists thought that the human brain was static and did not change after a certain period of development; or perhaps in the future when it is decided that the South Pole is actually the North Pole (haha).

A recently debunked scientific belief (that is actually still held by millions today) is the belief that we are at the mercy of inheriting bad genes and that if our parents had a disease, we are at equal risk of the same fate and there is not much we can do about it. This outdated paradigm and fear of our genes has been proven inaccurate through the new scientific study of epigenetics, which literally translates to 'control above genes.' Researchers discovered that genes are not in total control of health as was once thought because **genes cannot self-regulate**, which means they cannot act on their own. Scientists discovered that DNA is not set in stone as once thought because gene behavior is determined by signals from the environment and can only act once these signals have been received. "Genes cannot turn themselves on or off. In more scientific terms, genes are not 'self-emergent.' Something in the environment has to trigger gene activity." (Lipton, *The Biology of Belief,* xxiv) This discovery is monumental in what it means for our health, yet so few people even know about it. I still hear people say, 'I inherited my dad's bad back,' or 'My mom had a thyroid problem and migraines and now so do I.' The reason this may be so is actually entirely different from what we ever previously believed about genetics.

"We are living in a very interesting time with a new science called epigenetics. Epigenetics means how you think, how you feel, how you behave, how you speak can actually change the activity and expression of your genes. Only 5% of disease-related gene mutations are fully penetrant, which means you can't stop them. So when you think of the gene that Angelina Jolie had, that was a predictable gene, but the vast majority of disease-related gene expressions are influenced by your lifestyle."

~ Deepak Chopra

This idea that genes control life has been so deeply programmed into our psyches and culture that some scientists and the public have forgotten to keep in mind that genes controlling our health and disease was a hypothesis— not a proven fact.

For the sake of your health and understanding how the power of your thoughts, emotions, behavior, and beliefs directly affect your biology on a genetic level, let's briefly explore breakthroughs and discoveries in epigenetics, as this

information is essential to understand as you embark into the new, empowered paradigm of 21st century health and work to self-correct your anxiety.

I'll quickly review a very brief history of our evolutionary understanding of genes to make it clear how this mishap happened, as it paints a very similar picture to how you can make assumptions in your own life when judging certain evidence that can actually be proven incorrect upon further reflection, understanding, and investigation.

DNA: A Brief History

In 1910, scientists discovered that chromosomes within the cell held genetic hereditary information that was passed down to 'daughter' cells in the replication and dividing process. In 1944, it was recognized that the hereditary information within the chromosomes was DNA, but it wasn't until 1953 that DNA took its supreme title as the genetic ruler of human biology. James Watson and Francis Crick unraveled the double helix structure and discovered that DNA was subdivided into single genes, which held the blueprint information to build the entire body. The discovery was groundbreaking. "On Feb. 28, 1953, Francis Crick walked into the Eagle pub in Cambridge, England, and as James Watson later recalled, announced 'We have found the secret of life.'" (*Time Magazine*, 1999) Everyone thought Watson and Crick had hit the winning lottery on unlocking the mystery of the human body, and they were given the Nobel Prize in Physiology or Medicine for their discovery.

Their discovery was absolutely revolutionary; however, the histone proteins that the DNA tightly coils itself around were left out of this early research. Have you ever heard of histones? Most likely not...even though they are an *integral* component to how genes function. Why were they left out? Perhaps because histones are proteins, and because the human body is made up of over 120,000 different kinds of proteins, they might not have seemed as significant as compared to the complex and elegant structure of the DNA double helix. Conceivably, this might explain why they were left out of the early research of genetics, disease, and heredity.

Quite simply, scientists **hypothesized** that because DNA held the genetic blueprint to build the entire human body and created exact replicates of itself in the dividing process, the hypothesis was formed that all traits—desirable and undesirable—were set in stone, and that an individual was at the mercy of his/her inherited genes. But as time went by, gaps began to appear in this theory. For instance, each gene has sequence codes of RNA to build particular proteins in the body, which then build into different tissues to perform certain functions. At the start of the Human Genome Project, it was estimated that there would be at least 120,000 different genes to match the number of proteins in the body, but scientists were shocked to discover there were only 25,000 genes in the human genome! Something definitely didn't add up. Even more curious was when the number of human genes was compared to the number of genes in a worm:

"The primitive Caneorhbditis worm has precisely 969 cells and a simple brain of about 302 cells. Nonetheless, it consists of approximately 24,000 genes. The human body, comprised of over 50 trillion cells, contains only about 1,000 more genes than the lowly, spineless, thousand-celled microscopic worm." (Lipton, *The Biology of Belief*, 34)

How is it even be possible that a worm with fewer than 1,000 cells could have 24,000 genes and humans only have 25,000? This was the first clue that perhaps the Holy Grail of DNA wasn't all it was cracked up to be, as it was no longer possible for only 25,000 genes to fix, create, and build the complexity and function of the entire human body—*there simply aren't enough genes*.

Through this process, scientists went back to the drawing board to see if the histone proteins that the DNA wrapped itself around actually played an essential part in how genes operate. What they discovered was that histone proteins are incredibly important and elegant in their function, and are a crucial component in gene regulation in that they affect whether a gene is able to be read or not by uncoiling and uncovering DNA, thereby allowing the perfect gene sequence to be read in accordance with the required needs of the environment...which brings us to the field of epigenetics! Epigenetics, as mentioned earlier, translates to 'control above genes' and is the scientific study of understanding how signals from the *perceived* environment select, modify, and regulate gene activity.

Can you see why I am taking the time to teach you about epigenetics and to encourage you to understand your anxiety from a biological perspective? What we believe about ourselves and our environment directly impacts *how* we perceive ourselves and our environment (for better or for worse), and this perception impacts our gene function and our health. Your perception truly affects every cell of your body, and this means that that your physical health is directly connected to your emotional fitness and mental flexibility.

How do your perception and beliefs affect the readability of genes?

As said, DNA tightly coils itself around histones and, depending upon the spacing and structure of the histones, determines whether a gene is able to be read or not. For example, if the spacing is good, the genes can be read, but if the histones are coiled tightly, there is no way to access and read the gene. When a signal is picked up by the cell membrane from the environment (note: the cell membrane is a highly intelligent and evolved outer surface of each cell), it sends specific information into the histones within the nucleus, communicating if a gene needs to be turned on or off or what genetic sequence is needed to be read in order to create specific proteins in the body to match the needs of the environment. If a gene is partially covered, it leads to a variation in gene expression.

Dr. Lissa Rankin, MD, speaks about variations in gene expression in her book, *Mind Over Medicine*. She had become discouraged by what she calls 'our broken health-care system' and was determined to discover why some patients experience miraculous healings from seemingly incurable diseases, while others remain sick even when given medicine that should have cured them. In her book, she speaks about how epigenetics is revolutionizing our modern understanding of health and disease:

"We now know that each of these 25,000 genes can express itself in at least 30,000 ways via regulatory proteins that are influenced by environmental signals. Do the math. Studies have even shown that environmental factors can override certain genetic mutations, effectively changing how the DNA is expressed. These altered genes can then be passed down to offspring, allowing offspring to express healthier characteristics, even though they still carry the genetic mutation. The study of epigenetic control is revolutionizing how we think about genes. We used to think that some people were blessed with good genes while others were cursed with what some in the medical community insensitively referred to as 'piss-poor-protoplasm.' In fact, few diseases result from a single gene mutation. Less than 2% of diseases such as cystic fibrosis, Huntington's Correa, Beta Thalacemia, result from a single faulty gene. Only about 5% of cancer and cardiac disease patients can attribute their disease to heredity. Scientists are now learning that the genome is far more responsive to the environment of the cell

*than genetic determinism suggests. This means that the
majority of disease processes can be explained by
environmental factors to which the cells are exposed."*
(Lissa Rankin, MD, Mind over Medicine, Audio Book)

As we have seen, your beliefs effects how you react to your environment, and now we are learning that your environment directly impacts the function of your genes. But how does this work? How do your beliefs and thoughts affect your genes?

Each one of your cells has a cell membrane that acts as a microscopic perceiver in its environment, which means there are 50 trillion perceivers reading the environment of your human body. You have a thriving micro-universe within you, make no mistake! Each cell has millions of receptor proteins on its membrane. "If you were to assign a different color to each of the receptors that scientists have identified, the average cell surface would appear as a multicolored mosaic of at least seventy different hues—50,000 of one type of receptor, 10,000 of another, 100,000 of a third and so forth. A typical neuron (nerve cell) may have millions of receptors on its surface." (Candace Pert, PhD., *Molecules of Emotion*, 22-23.) Each protein receptor within the membrane has an evolved intelligence that communicates through vibrations, shapes, and humming, and is responding to the environment that your senses are perceiving. "Just as our eyes, ears, nose, tongue, fingers, and skin act as sense organs, so too do the receptors, only on a cellular level. They hover in the membranes of your cells, dancing, and vibrating, waiting to pick up messages." (Pert, *Molecules of Emotion*, 23) Therefore, through your cell membrane, each cell is responding with a masterful, biological communication system to adequately take action in light of what is going on in 'your' perceived environment. I will humbly say, the more I learn about our human biology and the orchestration of what occurs in a single human cell (that is estimated to be made up of 100 trillion atoms), the more reverence I have for the intelligence of life within us, as well as feeling great hope and inspiration for what science is teaching us is possible for our future.

For, as we have seen, when it comes to genes, health, and disease, there is immeasurably more going on than meets the eye. Your genes are not set in stone; they are constantly adapting and evolving with your perception and interaction with life. And who is the key player in how you perceive and respond to life? Your doctor? Your parents? Your partner? Heck no!

You are the key player.

As I have said, it is not what happens to you, it is *how you perceive* what happens to you...and this realization takes on a whole new meaning when considering the information we just discussed, not just for your own life experience and choice of attitude, but also for how your perceptions and emotional fitness affects the biological health of your body. If your cells are working tirelessly on your behalf, twenty-four hours a day, you too have a vital role to play—how you *choose* to perceive and respond to life.

And this brings us full circle back to BELIEFS, because if beliefs shape what you believe to be true about yourself and the world, then your beliefs are the foundation of how you act and perceive in your environment. And how you respond to your environment is directly interpreted by your body on all levels, sending environmental signals directly into your genes. This means that beliefs affect not only your personality and response to life experiences; they also impact the internal landscape of your 50 trillion cells, your genes, and ultimately your health.

Now that I hopefully have your full attention on the power of beliefs, we will explore common beliefs correlated with anxiety, how they get created, and why limiting beliefs are hidden under every symptom in the body.

"I have come to believe that virtually all illness, if not psychosomatic in foundation, has a definite psychosomatic component. Recent technological innovations have allowed us to examine the molecular basis of the emotions and to begin to understand how the molecules of our emotions share intimate connections with, and are indeed inseparable from, our physiology. It is the emotions I have come to see that link mind and body. This more holistic approach complements the reductionist view, expanding it rather than replacing it, and offers a new way to think about health and disease—not just for us scientists, but for the lay person also."

~ Dr. Candace Pert

At the Core of Symptoms in the Body are Achilles Heel Limiting Beliefs

Regarding anxiety and other physical symptoms you may have, I am going to up the level of intensity from limiting beliefs to Achilles Heel limiting beliefs. Achilles Heel beliefs are different from your average nagging beliefs because they are highly sensitive with volatile emotional triggers fueling them. They are a reactionary area of weakness within you and flood your body with mental and emotional irrationality when set off. These Achilles Heel limiting beliefs are typically not easily undone because what birthed them and sustains them are neurologically recorded memories of stressful events, trapped emotions, and polarized perceptions. These unresolved past events create reservoirs of trapped emotions in your body, and because they haven't been resolved yet, they can still be fully charged and powerful years later, imprisoning you in a limiting and stress-inducing reality. Therefore, your body cannot lie, and its symptoms are directly communicating to you that within your body-mind there is unresolved stress that needs your attention. When you learn to listen to the body and translate the meaning within symptoms, suddenly you are not left with a disempowering diagnosis but rather an opportunity to resolve your symptoms from the inside out and, in so doing, change your life in meaningful, life-enhancing ways.

"You're not just a physical machine that makes thoughts, nor are you just thoughts that make a machine. You are the continuum of awareness called body-mind-spirit, and when you include all of these things in your lifestyle, it is not a chore. You are inspired to live a life where you experience every day a joyful energetic body, a restful alert mind and what we call a lightness of being—you are in the flow state."

~ Deepak Chopra

Let's look at symptoms from a 21st century health perspective, because in truth, symptoms are really *only* the tip of the iceberg. Your symptoms and intense emotions are a feedback alerting you to something bigger underneath the surface. Symptoms are what you can readily see, feel, and experience; however, the **cause** is below the surface with a meaningful and fortuitous tale to tell if you take the time to investigate.

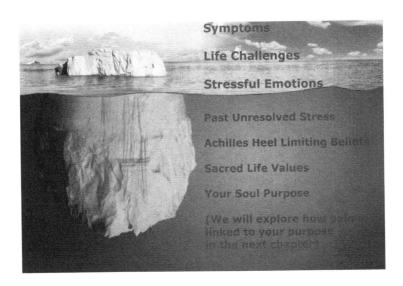

Symptoms

Life Challenges

Stressful Emotions

Past Unresolved Stress

Achilles Heel Limiting Beliefs

Sacred Life Values

Your Soul Purpose

(We will explore how beliefs are
linked to your purpose
in the next chapter.)

To understand why Achilles Heel beliefs are incredibly powerful, let's use our analogy from the previous chapter of a dam, but this time in your mind's eye picture the Hoover Dam. Now, behind the Hoover Dam are quadrillions of pounds of pressure. It took time for the reservoir to fill up, but as it did, the pressure began to build, and once full, the force behind the dam was enormous. Achilles Heel limiting-beliefs are like a mighty dam; they have an accumulation of trapped emotional kinetic energy behind them, and once these Achilles Heel beliefs are triggered, an **overwhelming** amount of emotional energy gets released inside an individual, temporarily overtaking his/her logical, reasoning mind. Have you ever gotten triggered and had your emotions completely take you over, causing you to react in the heat of the moment? Have you ever worried irrationally and were unable to stop? Have you ever felt an illogical response rise within you because of what someone said or did? If you are a human being, you should be nodding your head right now. Let's all nod our heads together, shall we?

Emotions are incredibly powerful. They are deeply important, creating beautiful depth and meaning within your life...but keep in mind that they are not the WHOLE of who you are. You can be a slave to your emotions if you give them your power, allowing your life and decisions to constantly be ruled *by* them. I personally don't believe we are here to be ruled by neurotransmitters (molecules of emotion) 100% of the time; rather, I believe we are to learn how to enjoy our emotions and *use* them consciously for our greatest good by understanding that they are a biological feedback of our internal and external environment. Your emotions are honest messengers, and when you stop and choose to get curious and listen to them, stopping for a moment to let go of your attachment to your story that is triggering your intense feelings, you will discover that your strong emotions have a treasure chest of information, wisdom, and purpose to share with you. One of which is that it is your acute emotions alert you to your Achilles Heel track pattern.

As previously described, a track pattern typically forms in childhood after you experienced a stressful event, which then created a lens of how you perceived and reacted to future challenges (similar or otherwise). As you accumulated more experiences, your Achilles Heel limiting belief strengthened, as well as corresponding negative self-talk, creating the cause and effect of excessive stress followed by physical symptoms. Integrative Health stops this cycle and empowers individuals with knowledge to pull back and understand what is happening and how to resolve this pattern. I am assuming you don't want your life to be imprisoned by track patterns and ever-fluctuating highs and lows of emotional hangovers, but rather to learn how to use your emotions as valuable teachers and powerful fuel to change your life.

The key then is to get to the root of where your Achilles Heel stress originated from and to understand what is holding your anxiety program in place. From here, to loosen the grip of your symptoms, you need to loosen the grip of your associated *story* of past stress, unravel the track pattern that you are on, and be open to the possibility that you might have experienced a stress from the perspective of a child as an all or nothing, black-or-white experience, when in truth, nothing is ever just black or white (and this perspective can massively keep you stuck as an adult). To move forward, be free of the past, and self-heal your symptoms from the inside out, you have to be ready and willing to look at your history from a 365-degree perception of wisdom and not just 1 degree of pain. The next chapter will be dedicated to loosening the disempowering grip of your old story and teaching you how to elevate it to an empowering one.

Before we end on this topic, I want to share that none of this is *bad*. It is a refinement process of our evolutionary journey. Two hundred years ago, we did not have the luxury to meditate on our emotions of how our childhood stress could lead to symptoms—we were in survival mode. Now however, millions have more time and security to reflect and learn, grow, evolve, question, and change their unhealthy behaviors. And interestingly, or rather quite beautifully, the implications of this appear to have a global impact. A theory within the Integrative Health community, through the scientific understanding that consciousness plays a direct role in health and disease, is that track patterns have perhaps a higher evolutionary purpose, that they are not only 'bad' but rather are essential physical symptomatic limitations to foster conscious growth that organisms or species must *evolve through* in order to continue to survive and thrive. When looking at health from the level of a *human being*, not just a human body, it demands that we take personal responsibility for our mental and emotional states of consciousness. In so doing, we are challenged as a species to grow wiser and more mature. And to decrease our stress, we must learn to evolve out of our inner child reactionary patterns to higher strategies of how we process stress; to learn how to come more from understanding, humility, compassion, wisdom, and love, rather than protection, resentment, fear, ignorance, and resentment. And in order to have greater emotional fitness, we are pushed to take into account the *whole picture* rather than seeing things from only a singular perspective where we defend ourselves if we feel we've be wronged. As the human population continues to grow in numbers, can you see how symptoms and disease might actually be a hidden, embedded intelligence within our biology, *forcing us to evolve*? To coexist on this planet for thousands of years to come, would you agree that human consciousness must progress if we are to find a new level of cooperation? First, we need to figure out how to do this individually, then with people we love, expanding outward into our work environment, community, country, and beyond. It is a compelling theory to contemplate how your individual symptoms could actually be interconnected with the whole of our global society, as well as future generations.

This is quite a big difference in perspective than just wanting to make your symptoms go away with a quick fix, or thinking you are stuck with anxiety for the rest of your life. In truth, there are many inspiring levels within Integrative Health, and the further down the rabbit hole you go, the more humbled and inspired you might become.

Now, in an effort to regain your power from anxiety limiting track patterns, let's investigate more deeply what unhealthy beliefs and behaviors might be holding you back due to early, unresolved childhood stress. Let's make your unconscious conscious!

4

Adaptive Anxiety Behaviors

You now have a greater understanding of how stress creates limiting beliefs, how this leads to a track pattern of repeating stress, and how this can eventually lead to physical symptoms in the body, so now let's get very clear on what unhealthy behavioral patterns might stem from these fears, as they will vary depending on what type of stress you were exposed to.

Growing Up with Addiction and/or Abuse

In our case study where an individual grew up with an alcoholic parent, a mentally ill parent, or a threatening parent, a stressful limiting belief might be, "Bad things always happen. I can't let down my guard because good things don't last. I am not safe." (Emotions matching these beliefs are worry, anxiety, frustration, and fear.) Children who grew up where a parent or parents had unpredictable outbursts of behavior can develop stress patterns of being on edge and not knowing what to expect on a day-to-day basis. Some days or weeks, everything appears to be okay, life is good, when suddenly everything comes crashing to the ground. Perhaps a parent loses control and lashes out at his/her kids in pain and anger; perhaps a parent had something bad happen at work and the whole family is put on edge by the palpable emotions of the parent's unpredictable, uncontrollable emotions.

This unstable childhood environment can create a number of stress-inducing behaviors:

- Needing to be perfect to avoid getting in trouble
- Fear of authority figures
- Compulsive need to escape stressful environments
- Struggling with getting too close in an intimate relationship for fear of letting someone in and being vulnerable to getting deeply hurt again. This can lead to difficulty trusting others and can cause individuals to sabotage relationships and/or flee
- As an adult, one might develop addictive behaviors of drinking, using drugs, overeating, sex addiction, or lack of self-control with spending money as an adaptive strategy to escape and avoid suffering, discomfort, fear, pain, abandonment, or rejection. All of these addictions can be to numb unresolved pain trapped inside
- Individuals with addictive personalities can become dependent on partners to take care of them as they have a difficult time taking care of themselves and fear abandonment and loneliness
- Weekly or daily struggles with feeling powerless and/or stuck

- Victim mentality can create lack of responsibility with a default tendency to blame others, make excuses, justify, and bend the truth
- On the other end of the spectrum, a child may grow up quickly and become overly responsible, possibly taking care of a parent and developing superhero qualities, always trying to fix things, making sure everything is okay, and trying to heal, save, and fix others. These individuals can be very sensitive to their environment and hyperaware if things are 'off,' and they might become controlling to try to create an environment that feels safe
- When the 'superheroes' become adults, they can become workaholics and perfectionists, trying to do their best in everything, fueled by a deep sense of responsibility, awareness of others' needs, and what needs to be done. This energy can unconsciously be driven by a need to create order and security, as well as to feel significant
- In some cases, rather than becoming nitpickers, they assume the majority of responsibilities in relationships, becoming the enabler, and/or going above and beyond their role at work. They can burn the candle at both ends, unaware of their body's needs or signs to slow down, run by people-pleasing tendencies in order to avoid conflict
- They can have unhealthy boundaries of giving too much, compromising, and completely getting sidetracked from their own needs because it is easier to help, save, and fix someone other than themselves
- Focusing on themselves brings up anxiety and fears of not being good enough

- Often they are attracted to partners for whom they mistake pity for deep feelings of love •For reasons beyond their conscious understanding, they deeply want to help their partner and/or feel obligated to, even if it means compromising their own health, happiness, friendships, career, and finances. They will stay in these codependent relationships because they see the good and *potential* in their partner; however, it is often fueled by the unconscious need of the enabler to feel valuable or significant by helping/saving their partner. (This powerful desire can be due to unconscious wounds, feeling like if they could save their parent, their parent might finally be happy and able to love and see them. That is why you will often find an addict with an enabler—both are working out unresolved stress from childhood, and both individuals need self-healing work—not just the addict.)

If any of the above sounds familiar for you, even if you didn't have a parent with an addiction, but they had mental illness or were abusive in some way, a great workbook I highly recommend on Amazon is: *Twelve Steps of Adult Children* http://www.amazon.com/Twelve-Steps-Adult-Children-Workbook/dp/0978979710. One of my clients described it perfectly when she realized that many of her character traits, which she had previously identified as being unique to her, were actually textbook survival traits from growing up in an abusive household. When you understand *why* you are doing what you are doing, you can update your strategies to be rooted in self-love and health, rather than being unconsciously run by fear and stress. Make sense?

The common character traits listed on the *Twelve Steps of Adult Children* cover are mistrust, procrastination, alcoholism, para-alcoholism (codependents), isolation, self-sacrificial, approval-seekers, terrified of abandonment, confuse love with pity, afraid of people and authority, self-centeredness, addictive lives, stuff feelings, perfectionism, judging self harshly, and addicted to excitement. If any of this sounds familiar, definitely look into getting the workbook and/or joining an ACA, *Adult Children of Alcoholics,* group similar to AA or Alanon. Even if you didn't grow up with addiction, but you were abused mentally, emotionally, physically, and/or sexually, you will greatly benefit from learning about the unconscious adaptive survival strategies that create codependent behaviors in relationships both personal and professional, as well as unwanted stressful experiences. Not everyone who has anxiety struggles with codependency/enabling, but if any of these points hit home, I suggest you explore this topic more thoroughly. Another book I recommend is *Codependent No More*, written by Melody Beattie.

Adaptive Unhealthy Behaviors - Growing Up with a Very Strict Parent and/or Perfectionist

In our other case study, where a child over the course of eighteen or so years was exposed to an environment where he/she experienced harsh or critical demands to get good grades, this repeated stress could easily create a conscious and unconscious inner-narrative of "I have to be perfect and do this perfectly. I can't mess up or else I'll get in trouble." (Emotions matching these thoughts would be obsessive worry, tension, and fear, and being gripped by a feeling of needing to be in control.) Imagine the mental and emotional stress of having to be perfect all the time—in everything. Perfect grades, perfect at sports, perfect room, perfect outer appearance, etc. I have worked with individuals who have repeated memories of extreme reprimand for doing 'poorly' on a test (a B+ for example), getting verbally and sometimes physically abused for not getting an A. Having a critical parent who was not necessarily a perfectionist but was very strict can lead to similar adaptive fears of "I can't mess up. I have to do this perfectly."

'I have to be perfect' is an incredibly challenging and exhausting belief to be run by every day. Often, individuals who hold themselves to this impossible standard:

- Can be hypercontrolling and self-critical, often running on anxiety to make sure they do everything flawlessly
- Become workaholics, burning the candle at both ends and tuning out their body's needs and physical symptoms
- Suffer with anxiety, insomnia, digestive problems, headaches, panic attacks, adrenal fatigue

- Are often incredibly hard on themselves, even to the point of self-loathing
- Have a fear of letting others close to them due to intense worry of others seeing their imperfections
- Have an obsession with their outer image and appearance
- Are afraid to go after what they really want to do in their lives
- Feel hollow on the inside, trying to maintain this perfect outside persona
- Exhaust themselves because of inability to say 'no'
- Have a fear of being unlovable
- Have a fear of losing control
- Don't know who they really are as they strive to be the person their parents and/or society wants them to be
- Can become compulsive cleaning fanatics, needing to have everything just so. If things are out of order, it can cause a great deal of tension and angst
- Run by their to-do list rather than enjoying being with others
- Need things done their way – cooking, cleaning, schedule, etc.
- Are unable to fully enjoy life or the journey because they are either looking ahead to the next task that needs to be done, or feeling anxious about what is not perfect at work, at home, with their relationship, physical image, car, finances, or anything else that they believe needs improving, which can typically include anything and everything
- Overparent by trying to be the super parent to a degree that is over-the-top and counterproductive

- Spend an imbalanced number of hours making sure everything is done impeccably and cannot rest until everything is finished on their to-do list. Often the consequences of this unconscious belief can have a negative spillover effect upon their romantic partnerships, professional affairs, and/or parenting as they expect everyone to live up to *their* standards and how *they* want things done (which is usually impossible for themselves, let alone for others)
- Often nit-pick and nag those closest to them, which can quickly strain and burden relationships, shutting partners down, kids down, and friends down, throwing the perfectionist deeper down into a spiral of anxiety run by the unconscious belief, 'I am not enough.'

The need to be in control and to avoid what you don't want can inherently create an imbalance of inner tension and cause negative results. The underlying need to be in control and/or have everything done to an extremely high self-imposed specification causes the hypercritical mind to rule the roost, and if those close to you fall short of the mark (which they will), you may get caught in criticizing and shutting loved ones down. After a while, being the commander of control can cause stress, tension, anxiety, insomnia, headaches, adrenal fatigue, ulcers, frustration, or anger, while simultaneously hurting people, making them feel smothered with constant criticism and feelings of never being good enough. If any of this sounds familiar, you can pull back and reflect if this is *what you really want*—to have things *your* way but at the price of inner tension and regular conflict with loved ones.

"The individual may strive after perfection, but must suffer from the opposite of his intentions for the sake of his own completeness."

~ Carl Jung

Don't worry if you are thinking, "Yes, this is me. Now what am I supposed to do?" The first step is identifying the problem. The second step is understanding why you are doing what you are doing. The third is resolving the stress that caused a problematic habit in the first place. The fourth is consciously creating a new way of being that feels inspiring and empowering for you. Also, please make a note that none of this is 'bad'—on a deeper level it is an opportunity for growth in ways that are both uplifting and life changing. **I love working with individuals who struggle with this conflict because once they learn how to harness this energy wisely, in a healthy, balanced way, there is nothing that they can't achieve.**

Common Anxiety Belief: 'I'm not good enough'

This is a universal belief I find 99.99% of my clients, my friends, my family members, and pretty much all of humanity having and being held back by in life. (Many are completely unaware of this because this belief is often unconscious; however, I find it consistently at the core of individual's deepest fears and wounds again and again when we get to the heart of the matter.) This common and deeply embedded belief of 'I'm not good enough' doesn't always have a tragic event attached to it, either; rather, it can be an accumulation of common occurrences and daily stress that build the wounds of self-doubt and fear over time. For example, have you ever been rejected? If you said 'no,' my eyebrows just raised as you'd have to be the only person on the planet who hasn't been! Rejection is *huge*, especially during your highly emotional, volatile, and hormonal adolescent years. Remember the sting of being rejected by your school crush? Or being rejected by a group of peers? Social rejection can be devastating. You feel it in the pit of your stomach, and it is imprisoning. Kids compare everything they have to their peers—their clothes, their grades, their houses, their phones, etc.

Think back on the thousands of homework assignments and exams you were graded on during thirteen to seventeen years of schooling. Five days a week, year after year, you experienced countless opportunities to feel like you failed and were not good enough while constantly comparing yourself to others. You weren't developing. You were over-developing. You wore glasses. You had acne. You didn't get asked to dance at the prom. You asked someone and he/she said 'no.' You got pantsed during recess. You made a stupid comment in class and everyone laughed at you. You scored the winning goal for the opposing team. You failed an exam and got ridiculed. Your coach forgot to tell you that you weren't suiting up for the varsity basketball game and, standing in your uniform in the center of the gym, alone and in front of the whole school after everyone else's name had been called, you waited to have your name announced so the crowd could cheer and you could run up and high-five your teammates...and after an *excruciatingly* long, awkward silence with an auditorium filled with hundreds of people (so quiet you could hear a pin drop), your best friend shouted out your name from the bleachers, followed by an awkward applause from the crowd as you ran to join your teammates with your face matching the bright red color of your uniform. (Yeah, that one actually happened to me! I turned in my uniform directly following the game. That shame ended my mad dribbling skills and basketball career, but that's okay because I rocked the soccer field. My senior year, I scored a goal and my coach posted in the local paper saying that I finally did it! Oh man, we have to laugh at ourselves because really it is too funny and you cannot make this schtuff up!)

The list goes on and on of why we all are trapped by the guttural fear of, 'I'm not good enough.' It is highly unlikely that you will ever find a single person who doesn't have some wound around this or who doesn't still harbor some abrasion of social or romantic rejection; yet we take it so personally, thinking we are the only ones who feel this way and thus try to hide it to protect ourselves so no one knows how vulnerable we feel. We allow the sting of rejection and failure to block us from sharing our true authentic selves, our gifts, and our light. This fear easily grips us well into adulthood, if not forever, unless this belief is cleared and, in many cases, comically laughed at for its many humorous origins. Maybe I could start a forum on my website where we could all share our most embarrassing moments and learn from one another that we are, in fact, not the only ones to have felt humiliation or rejection, and get over the sting so we can have the courage to really live.

On a side note: I feel I need to stress an important point. Children will form limiting beliefs no matter how balanced and perfect of a parent you intend to be or try to be. Stress is an inevitable part of life, and learning to deal with stress is a very important skill for your kids to develop. Additionally, there is great opportunity within every limitation for profound growth. So if you are a parent reading this and you are starting to feel guilty about challenging your kids, know that no matter what you do, your kids will form self-limiting beliefs and experience adversity in their childhood in some way, which really is a good thing because adult life typically has more than a few challenges, last I checked! Sheltering or overprotecting your children and spoiling them because you don't want them to feel pain can actually be more detrimental in the long run by robbing them of their independence and the opportunity to develop self-accountability, strength, and confidence in themselves to overcome emotional setbacks and challenges, which last I checked are all invaluable assets for later in life. Having greater independence and self-confidence is especially important when kids hit puberty and have to face the hormonal wrath of their peers without their parents there to protect them. (They typically don't want you hovering around as much anyway.) Additionally, not wanting to be too firm with your kids and letting them rule the roost, or being afraid to say no, can force someone other than you to do it—so even if you don't challenge them eventually, nature will balance out the equation, whether it is their peers, teachers, or other adults. Learning is a part of life through hard and soft lessons. If you want to empower your kids, be very present with them, give them consistent, healthy boundaries, and support them by saying how much you love them, how strong they are, how smart and capable they are, and regularly tell them how much you believe in them. Consciously plant **self-empowering beliefs over and over and over again** as this will greatly aid in building a solid foundation of high self-worth, self-love, and confidence, which will help them to overcome all forms of adversity and limiting beliefs later in life.

"Men often become what they believe themselves to be. If I believe I cannot do something, it makes me incapable of doing it. But when I believe I can, then I acquire the ability to do it even if I didn't have it in the beginning."

~ Mahatma Gandhi

A Big Anxiety Theme and a Look at Changing It

A big theme I see with individuals who have anxiety is a gripping need to be responsible and in control of pretty much everything: "I have a lot to do, and I have to be on top of everything because it is all up to me. I'll work however long and hard is necessary to get it how I want it, when I want it, and where I want it. I've got it. I can do it on my own. I don't need help." This individual is often compelled to work hard, perhaps unconsciously driven by how disempowered and out of control he/she felt when he/she was growing up with instability, unpredictability, outbursts of anger, stress, threat, or criticism, etc. This drive to work hard and be in control is a common modern day behavior, and it often does bring a return on investment, but I find it *excessively* out of balance with many people who have anxiety, adrenal fatigue, anger issues, physical pain, migraines, stomach ulcers, and/or those who suffer with insomnia.

Now, what might happen if these beliefs were adjusted slightly? "I work every day, focus clearly, and take balanced action toward what I want. Then I loosen the reins a bit and trust that life will support me. I recognize I am not doing this all on my own. I take the good with the bad. I practice flexibility, as I know everything works out in the end, and I will be okay. I work hard, but I equally love and enjoy the journey of my life."

108

Let's look at the difference between these two beliefs.

One belief is rooted in *control* while the other is rooted in *trust*. One belief *drives* an individual to feel, "I have to do it all on my own," while the other *sustains* the individual to feel, "I am supported every day in unexpected and beneficial ways." These two examples are just beliefs, plain and simple, yet they yield dramatically different behaviors, stress levels, and results. What we focus on and believe is what we allow ourselves to *see* and *experience,* and what we experience affirms our reality, which doesn't mean it's 'how life is'; it just means that that is what we are tuning in to more and thus what we will experience our reality to be like.

From personal experience, I can tell you that I used to be ruled by the belief of the first option above—being in hyper-control. My intentions were genuine and pure; however, it was ultimately self-limiting and frustrating. I did my best and worked really hard for years and years...until I finally got hit with a big lesson and realized that underneath my good intentions, I was really driven by a place of fear (which is why I needed to try to control everything), and thus I was restricting and blocking any consistent grace and effortless support from flowing into my life. **I was stuck in the illusion that everything was up to me, and if I wanted something, I had to work really hard and control the details of how that would happen. I believed deep down (unconsciously at the time) that I was doing it all on my own, and I used my determined WILL to make things happen (hence a little imbalance in my adrenals).**

A trauma occurred in my life that forced me to stop and reevaluate this limiting strategy for living. I will share more details shortly, but first I would like to say that since shifting my belief system toward the second option—trust—my life now flows with regular grace and support. I am not being new-agey here or airy-fairy. Trust me. My belief has changed so I have changed and my life along with it. I am much more appreciative in my life and aware of when grace happens now. I don't minimize support, push it away, or block it out because I am tuned into that this is *how life can be*, so I *allow* more support. I *allow* myself to receive more. Do you ever have trouble receiving? Life can be a lot harder when you block out support and don't allow others to help you or you don't feel comfortable receiving unexpected grace. Updating my belief, I feel safer and more secure as well. I have more fun. I don't feel like I am doing it all on my own with the weight of the world on my shoulders because I know this is not even close to true, and I completely trust in the process of my life unfolding, allowing opportunities to support me in ways I could not orchestrate nor conceive on my own. Now, when life brings me a challenge, I don't reject it or label it as a bad thing, rather I embrace it as an opportunity to grow stronger. More specifically, I allow the challenge to teach me what I need to learn so that I may develop more into my true self. I am grounded in the knowing that within every challenge there is also grace, even if it remains hidden for a while. Letting go of the unconscious, anxious need to feel in control, I have more space to enjoy the journey of my life, being more present with others heart-to-heart, rather than feeling a great responsibility for the horrible things going on in the world that I used to feel compelled to help solve, driven by a sense of impending immediacy.

Keep in mind I am still very much aware of what is going on in the world and seek daily to develop my ability to make a contribution to the areas I most care about on a global scale, but now this worry doesn't affect my health and well-being. I feel more grounded and I can now put my energy more effectively into solutions, rather than unconsciously running myself ragged. A micro-shift in perspective created a massive ripple effect. As one strategy is sustainable, while the other is not. One is a supportive, full of life, joy and humbling beauty, while the other is not. I still work and focus, but it is with a balance of ease and effort, rather than mostly effort.

Consider for a moment: Where might you be able to soften and find your breath within the intensity and stress of your life?

"Can you relax within the intensity of your effort?"

~ Yoga Sutra

Can you dance within the polar opposites and find the sweet spot between ease and effort, will and grace? Can you allow yourself to receive more? If you have a slew of health symptoms, then your body is probably hoping that you are open to the idea.

How Not Being in Control of Everything...is a Grace

If you have ever stood in the ocean where the waves break, you know the futility of trying to control the power of the sea and are instantly humbled by its greater force. The anxious human mind wants to act as though it is in control of much more than it is, when the truth is that there is only a small percentage of your life that *you are totally in control of*—such as how you choose to perceive challenges, what actions you want to take on to build your dreams and goals, how you choose to communicate, and how you treat others and yourself.

Now you may be thinking, "This is great, Bella. I am glad you trust and see more support in your life, but my life is hard, and I don't think this is a matter of belief. In fact, I *know* life is hard." If you are thinking this, you're right. Life is definitely challenging, and me telling you to see how much life is really supporting you and to trust this support more is good in theory, but you have to know and experience it for yourself. So let's look at that now, because the truth is that you are being supported by life—it is already happening—you only need to acknowledge how much and lose the illusion otherwise.

Let's get practical and take a look...

For instance, are you personally making sure that the roads you drive on are paved? Are you drilling for oil to fuel your car to simply drive to the store and buy food without having to grow or butcher it, allowing you to conveniently fill your fridge and cook your food on a stove that simply needs to be turned on? These may seem obvious, but we often take for granted how much we are supported in life. Yet, your mental and emotional well-being is 100% tied to your perspective about life...so let's get humble and really take a look at how much you are actually supported.

What about your clothes? Are you out in the cotton fields doing hard labor, picking the cotton to turn into cloth and then make your clothes? Are you responsible for forging the creation of photons in the sun to give light, heat, and life to this planet? Are you spinning the earth 67,000 mph around the sun, creating our experience of seasons, night, and day, and romantic sunsets or starlit nights? Did you build our moon to exact specifications for it to stabilize the earth's rotation on its axis, blessing us with consistent seasons, allowing us to grow food and inhabit the earth? Did you create the planet

Jupiter to watch over us by gravitationally pulling life-threatening asteroids into it rather than us? (An asteroid left a black mark the size of the Pacific Ocean after it crashed into Jupiter in 2009, and fifteen years before that, one left a black mark as big as the earth. If either of these two impacts had hit our planet, they would have ended life as we know it. Goodbye li'l things to stress about! When astronomers are looking for life in other solar systems, they first look for Jupiter-sized planets that act as a 'cosmic protector' to smaller planets capable of inhabiting life. Wow. Thanks, Jupiter! Glad I can delegate that one to you.) Are you beating your heart while you are reading this? Are you keeping your body alive while you are sleeping? Are you overseeing the proper function of the 200 billion cells in your brain?

Nope, you are not making any of these miracles happen, and you certainly are not doing it all on your own. Not even close! Rather, you are supported by *Life* every second. If you want to begin to dissolve the grip your anxiety has over you, one step is to expand your perspective to know how much you are supported, and the second is to humbly loosen your grip on thinking that you can be in control of every detail, and rather to *teach yourself* to appreciate how much you are supported, and turn the dial down on your need to be in control—down from a ten to a balanced five; you can control some things, but certainly not everything. Take a moment to reflect: are you minimizing where you are supported in life, while exaggerating micro-details of when things don't go exactly your way? If so, can you see how this sets the tone for a lot of stress, internal frustration, and being overly critical of oneself and others?

What do you consciously want your focus to be?

If your focus and belief is that 'life is hard, nothing works, and you have to do it all by yourself'—well you just might be stressed out a lot of the time. If your focus is, 'I am supported every day, I take the good with the bad because things have a way of working out for the best'—this focus might be a little more fun and support your long-term health. Actually, optimism is scientifically proven to be better for your health. "Optimists live longer than pessimists! That's the conclusion of a 30-year study involving 447 people that was conducted by scientists at the Mayo Clinic. They found that optimists had around a 50% lower risk of early death than pessimists and wrote that '...mind and body are linked and attitude has an impact on the final outcome—death.' A startling statistic. Optimists were also found to have fewer physical and emotional health problems, less pain, and increased energy, and they generally felt more peaceful, happier, and calmer than the pessimists." (David R. Hamilton PhD, How Your Mind Can Heal Your Body, 3).

Know that a micro-shift in perspective can make a world of difference. I invite you now to come up with a list of your own of 100+ examples of **how you are supported in your life without any direct effort or control on your part, and how people and life circumstances profoundly support you on a daily basis. Open your mind to the truth. See it for yourself. Expand your awareness and be prepared to feel a humble peace wash over you as you begin to acknowledge how much you are supported.** Calm your tense mind down and awaken your heart and mind to the grace that supports you each and every day.

"Trade your expectations for appreciation."

~Anthony Robbins

If you resist giving up the driving force of control, know that it may be because you like it. You are in charge. It can feel safer and more comfortable. You get to shape and influence things to be *your* way. And I acknowledge that sometimes there is absolutely a legitimate time and place to hunker down, work like crazy, and push yourself harder than you knew you could, and control the details with a magnifying glass (this book wasn't written while I was sunbathing on the beach drinking a Mai Tai in Hawaii, for example!). But know that if you drive life hard *every day* as a habit, with a gripping tension for years on end, this intensity comes with a high price that will affect your health, your relationships, and your joy in life—and life will feel unfair and hard because you are reinforcing it to be that way...every day. The truth is that it is not necessary to grip so tightly all the time, but first you'll have to have a heart-to-heart with your ego about loosening the reigns.

A Course in Miracles poetically illustrates this inner malady:

"This fragment of your mind is such a tiny part of it that could you but appreciate the whole, you would see instantly that it is like the smallest sun beam to the sun, or like the faintest ripple on the surface of the ocean. In its amazing arrogance, this tiny sunbeam has decided that it is the sun. This almost imperceptible ripple hails itself as the ocean! Think how alone and frightened is this little thought, this infinitesimally small illusion holding itself apart and against the universe. Do not accept this little fenced off aspect of yourself as yourself. The sun and the ocean are as nothing beside what you are."

I will finish this important topic by sharing that, for me, by learning to let go of the feeling that I needed to make everything work all of the time, I now have a new space and balance to truly breathe and appreciate the amazing gift that is my life. I have a humble and fulfilling awareness that I am alive on a rare, blue, beautiful planet, spinning around a star somewhere in an inconceivably infinite universe or perhaps even multiverse. One simple belief that 'life supports me - I trust life,' changed everything for me. But how I came to this understanding was through incredible pain.

During a late winter night, I was sleeping alone on a loft in my house. I had a stressful dream and while I was still sleeping, I got up and literally ran off my loft and fell nine feet onto my left sacrum and foot. The loud sound of my body hitting the hard floor, the cry that I let out, and the pain that shot through my entire body woke me up in agony. I cannot convey to you the intensity of the pain that tore through me. It was so bad that I began to hyperventilate, crawled to the bathroom, and threw up. Barely able to stand, I took a shower to try to warm my body that was ice cold and shaking due to shock. I felt so scared and heartbroken that I had hurt myself this badly. How could I have actually done this to myself? Not wanting to bother anyone at 1 am, I got an ice pack out of the freezer and somehow managed to climb back up my ladder and into my loft where I kept my zero-degree sleeping bag. Without any aspirin, I somehow got enough relief from the ice pack and drifted in and out of sleep until 5 am when I could call one of my best friends who lived on the East Coast. The next morning, my mom was so upset and asked me why hadn't I called her. *Yeah, why hadn't I?*

It took this nine-foot fall for me to finally shake loose from my ego that was pushing so hard and realize that there had to be a better way to live my life. This challenge and injury forced me to surrender my false sense of control...but even then, I was still holding on, fighting to be strong, using my WILL to make everything okay, so that trauma still wasn't enough. The injury was compounded by another shocking crisis that happened a few days later in my family that pushed me to a critical point in my existence, forcing me, if you will, to open to grace. For the first time in my life, I trusted I would be supported through something other than by my own will making it happen, because I couldn't do it on my own anymore. And how I was 'doing it' obviously wasn't working that well. I realized that there had to be a better way. I came to a place of acceptance, humbly surrendered, and opened to grace. I took a big step into my fear, and I let go and trusted that the force giving me life and supporting me in so many ways would catch me.

For the first time in my life, I *truly surrendered*. And what held me in my surrender was far more beautiful than anything of earthly security...day by day I began to learn that grace *was real*. Unexpected opportunities came to me in supportive and even miraculous ways and continued to do so. This period was one of the most painful, humbling, and scary times of my life...but it was also one of the most profound, healing, and transformative periods of growth that changed the course of my life forever. I don't live by force anymore; I live by humility, trust, patience, and confidence. It is a good combination. And one of the many gifts of this experience is that I can share this lesson with you. In the modern, fast-paced world, we grip so tightly and take ourselves and the details so damn seriously. In so doing, we lose track of the bigger picture, greatly limit and burden ourselves, and accumulate excessive, unnecessary stress, frustration, and struggle rather than filling our days with greater appreciation, serenity, enjoyment, and fulfillment. If you can learn to let yourself ease up on the reins a little bit and soften your narrow gaze, you will begin to see more clearly the miracles and abundance that support every moment of your remarkable life.

"If you would like to make an apple pie from scratch, you must first invent the universe."

~ Carl Sagan

5

Uncover Your Limiting Beliefs

You are probably curious about getting to the heart of your Achilles Heel beliefs—so let's look at this now. We will investigate through two exercises: First, a Kinesthetic (feeling) Exercise, and second, a Mental Exercise.

Intuitive Kinesthetic

Intuitive kinesthetic also means your emotional feeling intelligence. Your intuitive knowing that doesn't necessarily come through thought or logic, but is your feeling awareness that relays information. We will start with this, as your anxiety is a physiological feeling that is very powerful. The first step to solving a problem is identifying it.

First, you will want to have something to write with and then find a comfortable position.

Now, I invite you to come into the present moment and relax your mind and body. Let's get curious together for a moment...Let go of any pressure of expectation. There is no right way to do this. And trust whatever you get, okay?

Take a nice deep breath in and let out a long exhalation. Take in another full breath and let out another deep exhalation. Let it all go and come into the present moment. Breathe into just this moment, emptying yourself of thoughts and feelings that don't serve you, letting them simply fall away. Tilt your forehead gently upward toward peace and serenity, allowing your thoughts to easily slide out from the back of your head. Create space for silence and presence to come into your mind and body.

If you feel anxious, or if it is difficult to take a deep breath, and there is constriction in either your heart, solar plexus, or stomach, rest your healing hands on this tight spot in your body. Now with your hands resting on this restricted area, say to yourself, "Sometimes I feel overwhelmed," then breathe in...and exhale. "Sometimes I feel like I have to do it all by myself," then breathe in...now exhale. "Sometimes I feel like nothing ever works," then breathe in...and exhale. "Sometimes I feel that nothing I do is ever good enough," then breathe in...and exhale. "Sometimes I feel all alone," then breathe in...and exhale. Notice if any emotion comes up or if your breath was able to flow more easily by simply acknowledging the stress inside yourself. Now in a curious, calm, and quiet space...

Ask yourself:

"When I feel challenged or anxious, what is my belief about myself or about life? What do I believe deep down is true?"

Tune into your anxiety. If your anxiety had a voice, what would it say? What is *its* story? What is it afraid of?

Take a few minutes to intuitively connect with your anxiety and hear the belief that is your symptoms.

My Anxious Belief is:

Is this a belief that you would like to upgrade to a more supported, confident way of living? Remember, it is just a *belief*; it is not a fact. Yes, you have experienced stress and have an accumulation of evidence that makes you believe that your belief is 100% real, so what I am saying may scare you or upset you on a deep, instinctive level; however, I have been where you are. I understand. You are not alone in your feelings about this. Just know that if you are feeling any fear, anger, or resistance, this is the energy of past stress holding this belief in place. In this chapter, I simply want to introduce to you the possibility:

What if I have the power to shift my life and health for the better by shifting my core-limiting belief?

(Side Note: I was trained in Somatic Respiratory Integration. To learn more about the breathing technique above, Dr. Donald Epstein has an excellent book called *The 12 Stages of Healing*, which guides you through the twelve stages that individuals go through in the healing journey and includes powerful breathing exercises to release stress from your body within these stages. The first stage is suffering.)

Mental Exercise

Some people are more tuned into themselves emotionally, while others are more cerebral, and others are equally both. So now we will look to investigate your beliefs from a more left-brained, logical approach.

I invite you now to spend ten to fifteen minutes on this mental exercise where you can investigate what limiting beliefs might be controlling your behavior without you even realizing it.

Here are a few questions to make your unconscious conscious:

1. What is a big stress in your life right now?

(Perhaps you are dealing with a challenge at work, or with your partner, parents, finances, health, kids, etc.)

2. Now detach from your story a little bit and get curious. Does it feel like a familiar or ongoing challenge in some way? Is there a common theme on some levels?

Here are two examples to clarify:

a. You are feeling stressed and on-guard, like there is always some unexpected crisis you have to deal with. It seems like there is always a dramatic problem with either your family, your work, or your finances, and you can never let your guard down.

b. Perhaps you don't feel you are ever appreciated for all you do. For instance, you give and give at work and your boss doesn't recognize all your effort. And coincidentally, your partner doesn't appreciate all that you do either.

Investigate to see if this challenge is a repeating story in your life, perhaps with new characters?

3. Now what do you believe deep down to be true and hidden underneath this stress or challenging theme in your life? What do you believe about life or about yourself?

Find out what your unconscious, limiting belief is under your story and fear. Your belief is the description of how you feel. It is a simple statement. Make your unconscious conscious. This is so important.

For example:

a. Feeling there is always a crisis you have to handle could create the belief/reality:

"If it's not one thing, it's another." "Nothing works out for me." "Life is hard." "I have bad luck." "Something bad always happens." "I have to prepare for the worst." "I am not safe and secure." "Good things happen to *other* people." "Life sucks." "Life is unfair." "Nothing I do is ever good enough." "Something is wrong with me." "I'm being punished."

b. **Not feeling appreciated could create the belief/reality:**

"People don't appreciate me." "I am not seen." "I am invisible." "I am not wanted." "I am not loved for who I am." "I am not good enough." "Nothing I do is ever enough."

Side Note: Sometimes when you are investigating and trying to uncover a limiting belief, it can feel like none of the ones you are coming up with really hit the nail on the head. They don't really resonate as the heart of the issue. If you come up against a wall, don't worry, just keep exploring deeper. For instance: "I am not seen"….underneath this could be an even deeper, more sensitive belief of "I am unlovable," or "people don't see my worth." When you arrive and make conscious a limiting belief, *you will know it*. You will feel the energy. You will say, "Yes that is it." Connecting to your belief can make you feel raw or emotional or you can feel it so clearly that you recognize it as a 'truth' in that you can't imagine it being anything other than true.

4. When you find your limiting belief, see if you can create a little bit of distance from it and reflect:

a. Is this belief limiting me in a way I don't want? Is it causing me a great deal of stress, volatility, and undesirable experiences?

If it is limiting you, can you see that if deep down this is what you really believe to be true about life—that you will have to continue on this path? How could you not? This is *your powerful, definite belief* about the world and yourself, and this is how you will continue to feel, think, and filter reality. Make sense? Your belief is so real and powerful that it will be your blueprint and your default habitual reactionary program when you experience challenges.

Your belief will force you to stay on the same track pattern, seeing reality from its stressful, skewed lens—unless you have had enough, and *you choose* to change it.

Later in the book, we will talk about how to clear and upgrade your limiting beliefs, because even though they are just 'beliefs,' they have a lifetime of stressful experiences attached to them, which makes them powerful. And this powerful fuel can be used in a very positive way to self-heal and transform your life! As I said, life supports you in miraculous ways. So too is there light within your deepest challenge. There is a wise method I use to clear outdated beliefs and gain the gift they simultaneously contain. Finding this gift is at the heart of this book to help self-correct your anxiety from the inside out. But first let's not only focus on the negative side of beliefs; I want to briefly look at **Empowering Beliefs,** as they are EQUALLY powerful, inspiring, life-changing, and essential to understand to self-heal your anxiety.

Empowering beliefs

We have spent a great deal of time speaking about negative beliefs, so now I would love to discuss the flip side to this equation and explore the magic and power of empowering beliefs. Just as negative beliefs can hold you back, positive beliefs can launch your forward and set you free. Whether you know it or not, you have the ability to change your life in profound ways by consciously upgrading and evolving your beliefs to how you would prefer your life to be. This is legitimate. It is life changing to understand how powerful beliefs truly are, and that they can have an equally positive or negative impact on your life. This is why I am taking the time to really make this section clear, applicable, and logical for you. I want you to understand the power of beliefs beyond a concept. I want you to know their importance and consciously learn to use them positively in your life—and with certainty. To get started on the conversation, here is a medical case study from Harvard demonstrating the true power of the mind's ability to positively influence the body:

"Scientists from Harvard conducted a novel experiment in 1989. They took volunteers from over the age of 70 to a retreat center and asked them to act as though it was 1959 for over a week. The environment in the center was a recreation of 1959. Music from 1959 was played, there were magazines from 1959, the volunteers wore 1950s clothing, and the TV even showed taped shows from the 1950s. The volunteers had to converse with each other as though it was 1959, discussing topics and current affairs of the time.
"At the start, the scientists took a host of physiological measurements, including height, finger length, strength, mental cognition, and eyesight. After ten days in the center, they took those measurements again and discovered that the volunteers had gotten physiologically younger by several years just by acting as if they were younger. They grew taller, their fingers grew longer, they had improved mental function, and their eyesight had improved. Some of the volunteers had become mentally and physiologically younger

by 25 years." (Hamilton, *How Your Mind Can Heal Your Body,*
13-14)

Clearly, we have a conditioned perception of aging. We have unconsciously accepted that aging will be a certain way...but this study goes to show that we have the power to alter this 'reality' by actively perceiving differently.

"One of the things that is becoming very clear about the aging process is that what we consider normal aging maybe a premature cognitive commitment. We, as a species, get committed to a certain reality of aging."

~ Deepak Chopra

I am blessed to share with you from personal experience one of my family members who teaches the true power of beliefs when it comes to aging, or not aging, for that matter! Words such as elegant, noble, and sagacious were created to describe a woman like my grandmother. A couple of months ago, we were talking on the phone, as we often do, about a wide variety of subjects when she asked me how my birthday was. I told her, "It was so fun. We went to Water World and decided to literally play like kids, pretending we were teenagers, and we laughed hysterically all day." She replied, "Oh, that is great! Mentally, I feel young. I feel how I was when I was in my thirties and forties. I think if you're healthy in mind and spirit, you don't believe in age. I stopped believing in the age of my birthday years ago. I am not shy about telling people my age because I don't identify with it. They are just numbers to me." We had never talked about this before, and many in our family have often wondered how she continues to defy 'normal' aging. What you don't know is that my grandmother is 88 years old and still works full-time in Manhattan. She commutes five days a week into New York City and is the legal administrator for one of the top publishing companies in the United States. All the attorneys love her and tell her that she can't retire. In November of 2013, she celebrated her 50-year anniversary at her company (this would have been longer, but she started working as a secretary in her early forties after her four children went to school). This year she is feeling ready to retire and experience the next stage of life...I love hearing her talk about it. There is a sweet innocence...'You know I can sleep in. I am looking forward to that,' she says. I'll end by saying that my grandma is also stunningly beautiful, and you would presume she was much closer to 70 years old rather than approaching 90. Certainly, she is a testament to the power of beliefs that have helped shape her emotionally wise mind and a purpose-filled life; without question, she has been an amazing role model and has inspired me, my family, and hundreds who know her.

While I lived in London, I attended a seminar called "How Your Mind Can Heal your Body" with Dr. David Hamilton, a molecular biologist who formerly worked for the pharmaceutical companies creating prescription drugs. He did years of clinical trials testing the effectiveness of his potential drugs against placebos. Placebos are used as a control in a blind study where participants do not know if they are being given the real pill or a sugar/saline pill or injection. Placebos are not supposed to produce any healing effects whatsoever, but science is not always as cut and dried when it comes to dealing with a human *being* rather than just a human *body*. After witnessing miracle after miracle of the mind's ability to heal the body, Dr. Hamilton grew more inspired to share this scientific information with the masses and courageously chose to change his profession. Here is another case study from his book that reveals the mind's extraordinary power to heal the body and produce its own natural chemicals based purely on a belief:

"Since the advent of brain-imaging technology, there has been a surge of interest in the placebo effect. Research now shows that when we believe we are taking a drug but really it

*is a placebo, the brain lights up as if it really were taking the
drug and produces its own natural chemicals.*

*"This has recently been shown with Parkinson's disease.
The symptoms of Parkinson's disease arise from **impaired
production** of a substance called dopamine in part of the
brain. This affects movement. Research has shown that
Parkinson's patients given a placebo but told that it is an
anti-Parkinson's drug are able to move better. Brain scans
have shown that the brain is activated in the area that
controls movement and **dopamine is actually produced**. The
improved movement is not just a 'physiological' thing. It is a
physical release of dopamine in the brain."* (Hamilton, "How
Your Mind Can Heal Your Body," 20)

Profoundly, this study proved that what was impairing the
body's ability to produce dopamine was **not solely a physical
malady**, but that there must have also been a mental or
emotional component because when given the placebo, not
only was the patient able to move better, but the brain
actually produced dopamine, whereas before it could not.

What caused the brain to suddenly be able to produce
dopamine?

The human mind and spirit have proven through
thousands of clinical trials that it can create its own medicine,
and I believe that the more we work with this innate ability,
the more we can harness the true self-healing power within
ourselves. Here are Dr. Hamilton's own thoughts about
placebos and beliefs:

*"Designing and developing drugs is a painstaking and
highly skilled process that requires exceptional skill in
manipulating the chemical structure of molecules. But test
tubes don't involve human consciousness. Once a person
ingests a drug, that person's thoughts about the drug*

become all-important. The person is either going to believe that it will work or that it might not. But what they believe will affect how well the drug works...Placebos heal. That is a fact! But the real power comes from inside us. Placebos are symbols to which we attach our thoughts of hope or relief. The thoughts are ours. (Hamilton, *"How Your Mind Can Heal Your Body,"* 38)

The power of the human mind and spirit is boundless. The more we understand and work with this remarkable medicine and self-healing ability within ourselves, the less powerless we will feel about our physical symptoms and the more alive and **engaged** we will become in actively aligning with our bodies on mental, emotional, physical, and spiritual levels— to harness this remarkable, beautiful energy within.

Finding Sugar Man

While writing this book, I had the fortunate opportunity to see the documentary *Finding Sugar Man*. If you haven't seen this film, I highly recommend it. It is brilliant, and what's more, it beautifully illustrates the true power of beliefs and how a simple belief can help transform an entire country and start a cultural revolution. Throughout history, we have seen how ideas and beliefs change the course of destiny, giving rise to democracy, freedom, separation of church and state, equality, human rights, and recently, marriage equality. This film artistically and poetically demonstrates how the people of South Africa, who were oppressed and controlled by the policy of apartheid, finally gave themselves *permission* to rise against their country's governing power after hearing a revolutionary belief in a song from the album *Cold Fact* by Alex Rodriguez. Here is a transcription from the film:

*"I remember I was in high school, and we heard this song, 'I Wonder How Many Times You've Had Sex,' and at that time South Africa was very conservative. It was the height of apartheid, and there wasn't television. That is how conservative it was because television was communist. It was really, well you won't believe. Everything was restricted, everything was censored, and here is this guy singing this song 'I Wonder.' It was the big song we were all singing. The album was exceptionally popular. To many of us South Africans, it was the soundtrack to our lives...The message it had was be anti-establishment. And one of the songs is called 'Anti-Establishment Blues.' We didn't know what anti-establishment was until it popped up on a Rodriguez song. And then we found out it is okay to protest against your society, to be angry with your society. Because we lived in a society where every means was used to prevent apartheid from coming to an end, **this album somehow had lyrics that set us free as oppressed people.** Any revolution needs an anthem and in South Africa, Cold Fact was the album that gave people permission to free their minds and to start thinking differently...It had an enormous impact to make you just think that there is another way. What is presented to you by establishment isn't all there is."*

Again, I highly recommend watching the film if you haven't seen it yet, for it beautifully illustrates through an inspiring and remarkable true story how a micro-shift in perspective can result in such life-changing effects. Your beliefs give you permission to be yourself and do amazing things, or they can be the chains that hold you back. In this beautiful documentary, the true effects of beliefs are demonstrated within two opposing viewpoints: It is *not* okay to go against the establishment versus it *is* okay to go against the establishment. They took out a single word in their belief system, and started a cultural revolution.

Choose your beliefs and thoughts wisely.

They affect the construct of your reality.

Belief – Be Life

Although gravity is invisible, you can most certainly see its powerful effects. Beliefs are like gravity—beliefs are also invisible, and once you understand how deeply they impact your psyche and physiology, you will most definitely see their effects.

So the big question is how can you integrate this practical knowledge and begin to experience self-healing and freedom from your limiting-beliefs? How can you make this real and not just ideal? How can you actually clear deeply rooted, self-sabotaging chains with a lifetime worth of stress attached to them? How can you replace your limiting beliefs with empowering ones that you will actually *believe* and live your life from?

The answer is, in fact, much more beautiful than one might possibly expect and is at the very heart of this book, which leads us to our next chapter: **Pain to Purpose.**

6

Pain to Purpose

A Self-Healing Journey with a Gift in Disguise

"As my sufferings mounted, I soon realized that there were two ways in which I could respond to my situation— either to react with bitterness or seek to transform that suffering into a creative force. I decided to follow the latter course."

~ Martin Luther King Jr.

This is what we have been building towards. Everything I have been speaking about—META-Health, limiting beliefs, CT scans, track patterns—it all merges together into this focal point. This is why I am writing this book. To share with you a new, empowered perspective and opportunity within your anxiety—to foster a new understanding of what 21st century Integrative Health is about at its core. **Self-healing is the path that leads you back to the very heart of who you are by assisting you to integrate wisdom from suffering and learn**

how to transform those challenges into a creative, purposeful force. Indeed, a profound opportunity lies hidden within your anxiety to not only resolve your symptoms from the inside out, but in so doing, to awaken you to what you love and are most inspired by in life. And I don't mean this as a hyped concept of love. I am speaking about your *deeper Soul's Calling*—that which fills up your heart, inspires you, brings tears to your eyes, what you value most, what connects you to your truth, and what you feel called to do on this planet.

This is the actual opportunity available to you within your anxiety, past stress, and limiting beliefs. We want to use your pain and challenges as a force for tremendous good. For trapped and unresolved stress is not 'bad' energy; it is pure energy that you can turn into rungs on a ladder upon which you can climb.

This chapter will focus on how to resolve the unresolvable and set yourself free.

To do this, we will first begin by looking at pain and stress from a different light.

Pain to Purpose: How to Resolve the Unresolvable

"Challenge is a dragon with a gift in its mouth. Tame the dragon and the gift is yours."

~ Noela Evans

Your pain runs deep. It runs all the way through you into your innermost self and strikes a resounding chord that penetrates your heart, which is why you will consciously or unconsciously seek to heal it throughout your life. Therefore, although your wound may be painful, it simultaneously acts as a *sacred driver* to the very core of who you are and sets you

136

on a definite path—whether you are aware of it or not. Your wounds and pain cause a deep void or inner lack inside yourself, and because of that you will spend an entire lifetime trying to fill and solve this pain—which *is **why** it is so fulfilling and meaningful* to you on a heart level when you do. However, if you remain completely unaware of the sacred purpose that pain initiated in your life, you will continue to be run by emotional hangovers of unresolved, habitual worry, resentment, hurt, fear, anger, and stress—and your hurt will accumulate into symptoms in your body and keep you from embodying your true potential.

To solve this problem, the most effective path I know is to consciously learn, grow, and evolve through challenges confronting you by discovering how your greatest pain can actually help awaken you to what you love and value most in your life. I want to teach you how to use your emotional pain in a beneficial, enlightening way, for it has *invaluable* wisdom to share with you that you do not want to numb out, run from, or miss. In this chapter, I hope to help you begin to learn how to illuminate the hidden order of cause and effect in your own life and how to understand that pain and purpose are actually unified, interconnected units of energy; they are not separate forms of chaos, but rather invisible forces of order and meaning. When you find the meaning—you will know it. It will ring true to you on every level of who you are and simultaneously help you to resolve your anxiety.

"In some ways, suffering ceases to be suffering at the moment it finds a meaning. What man needs is not the discharge of tension at any cost, but the call of a potential meaning waiting to be fulfilled by him."

~ Viktor Frankl, Holocaust Survivor, Neurologist, Psychiatrist, Existential Analyst

By far, the most powerful and effective methodology that I have come across to transform suffering into meaning, and thereby resolve your anxiety, is the Demartini Method® created by Dr. John F. Demartini. What I deeply value about Demartini's work is that it is profoundly effective on even the *most* challenging experiences that other techniques don't seem to get to the absolute heart of. **Equal to the challenge is the blessing hidden within the crisis, and it is tremendously helpful to have a revolutionary tool to awaken your mind and heart to what that gift is.** The Demartini Method is the technique I use as the cornerstone of my practice and this process is what I see again and again assisting my clients to change their lives in profound ways. In truth, one of the reasons I am dedicated to writing this book is because I want as many people around the world to know that this modality is available and that long-term suffering is unnecessary. I grew up witnessing a family member suffer, and from a young age I knew somewhere deep within myself that the light of love and wisdom could resolve pain; this inner knowing initiated a core value within myself to find a way to integrate pain and darkness into love and wisdom, and at age nineteen, I began my journey into the healing arts. When I met Demartini, his methodology was the powerful and life-changing technique I had been seeking since I was a child. I am inspired to write this book to contribute to a new paradigm about health, disease, self-healing, and what is *truly* possible within the human heart and spirit.

In this chapter, I will go in depth into the teachings of his work, so that you may understand what is possible when you apply his method to your own life. The principles of his technique are simple and elegant. Yet, the simplicity asks that you go to a deep level within yourself and perceive the world with new eyes. For this reason, I think it is wise to give you a short background on Demartini and how the Demartini Method came to exist.

The Foundation of the Demartini Method

Demartini almost drowned at age seventeen when he became partially paralyzed from strychnine poisoning while surfing massive waves on Oahu's famous North Shore. He managed to make his way back to his tent and then blacked out. Three days later, he awoke on his near-deathbed, completely dehydrated and covered in vomit, urine, and excrement. Fortunately, a woman happened to be walking down a path through the jungle and heard him in distress. For three days, she nursed him back to health and then brought him to a health food store. On their way out, Demartini saw a flyer that read: "Yoga Class–Special guest speaker: Paul C. Bragg." Demartini felt a strong pull to go and try to heal his weakened and spasmodic body. When he met Paul Bragg, Demartini was amazed by how this older man was so healthy, strong, and full of life. Bragg spoke about Universal Laws, the importance of health, and having an inspired mind; he then led the class through a profound meditation to connect them to what they would love to dedicate their lives to doing. During this experience, Demartini suddenly had a crystal-clear vision, so clear it was as though it had already happened. In the vision, he saw that he would come to master and understand what Paul Bragg called Universal Laws, how these laws related to health and healing, and that he would share his findings with people all over the world. Even though his vision was so clear, in that moment, fulfilling the vision seemed improbable to him because at the age of seven, he had been identified as having dyslexia and was told he would never be able to read, write, communicate, or go very far in life. At fourteen, he had dropped out of school, left his home and family in Texas, and pursued his love of surfing; however, after escaping death by a thread and learning from a powerful teacher who embodied profound wisdom, exceptional health, and saw within his *true* potential, Demartini was determined to overcome his dyslexia and fulfill his own inspired calling to learn and teach.

Shortly thereafter, he left Hawaii and went home to Texas on a mission. His first step was to master reading and, with determination and dedication, he overcame his dyslexia. Because he had been unable to read through an entire book for the first seventeen years of his life, Demartini now had an insatiable appetite for knowledge and research. During his earlier studies, he happened upon a wise philosopher and mathematician named Gottfried Wilhelm von Leibniz. "I came across a great book by Gottfried Leibniz and it was called the *Discourse on Metaphysics.* In the first chapter, he said there was a divine perfection, a divine order, and a divine love, and for those individuals who somehow have a glimpse of this, their lives are changed forever. But the majority of the people, the masses if you will, don't. And they have no concept of this." (Transcription from *Personifying the Quantum Theory*) When Demartini read Leibniz's words, tears welled up from the depth of his being and he knew, "There has to be something significant here, and it's just a lack of our understanding that keeps us from acknowledging this hidden, divine order." (*The Breakthrough Experience*, 4)

Demartini began his quest to study over 280 different 'ologies.' Over time, he would speed-read more than 29,600 texts in his pursuit to glimpse the interconnected, underlying wisdom and intelligence seemingly governing all fields. "In my study of philosophy, religion, and science, I came across the term *logos*, which has many meanings, but essentially represents the source of all existence...ancient philosophers who were well-versed in all areas spoke of the *logos*—as a cohesive field of reason or intelligence. Today, we have specialization, so the *logos* that the great philosophers studied has fractionated into the various disciplines and 'ologies.' If you were to study all of the disciplines, however, you'd discover the common threads that make up the *logos*. That's why I wanted to tackle so many pieces of the puzzle myself—I wanted to see more of the whole picture." (Demartini, *Riches Within,* 148)

Moreover, Einstein's famous equation, $E = mc^2$ tells us that everything derives from a unifying source as well. Our bodies, the Earth, the sun, trees, oxygen, water, computers, thoughts, emotions, and spirit are all created from the same source— pure energy. Einstein's equation explains how energy can be transformed into mass and that both sides of the equation are two ways of looking at the same thing, which means E (*energy*) is the unifying 'medium' within all existence and to study *energy* is to unlock mysteries and discover infinite levels of Universal Laws and hidden order. Demartini wanted to understand how the laws of physics correlated to human consciousness and healing and to answer the greatest of philosophical questions:

Is there a purposeful, wise, loving intelligence permeating the universe?

From Demartini's four decades of research and working with hundreds of thousands of individuals from all around the world, here is a brief introduction into his methodology, the Demartini Method.

Physics, Consciousness, and Light

The Demartini Method is based on the fundamental laws of energy. To understand his method, we must delve into the basics of physics to have a framework upon which to build. I will be translating Demartini's research on the simplest level to make this section practical and easy to assimilate; Demartini himself has reviewed this section to ensure that I am describing his technique accurately. I feel it is important to say that, although I am not an expert in physics, I do love learning about it.

What is energy? What is this imponderable substance that gives life to the universe?

For hundreds of years, physicists have sought to understand energy at the fundamental level, and thus far, our technology has revealed the smallest measureable unit of electromagnetic energy to be a photon; or as renowned physicist Stephen Hawking describes a photon in *The Universe in a Nutshell*, "A photon is a quantum of light; the smallest packet of the electromagnetic field." String theorist Brian Greene defines a photon in his book, *The Elegant Universe,* as "the smallest bundle of light."

Physicists were perplexed when they discovered that a quantum of light is actually dualistic in nature—sometimes acting as a wave and sometimes acting like a particle. When a photon is in a wave state, it travels at the speed of light, exists in multiple places at once, is timeless, spaceless, chargeless, and massless; however, when a photon of light turns into mass, it transforms into two charged particles—a particle and an antiparticle. For example, an electron is a negatively charged particle and its paired antiparticle is the positively charged positron. **The two are inseparable and together they** make up one quantum of light; you can never have one without the other. "We now know that every particle has an antiparticle, with which it can annihilate." (Hawking, *The Illustrated A Brief History of Time,* 89) In this reference, 'annihilation' means that when the positive and negative paired particles find each other in time and space, they annihilate back into what Hawking describes as a "great flash of light." We will speak of the importance of paired particles turning back into light later in this chapter and how this relates to your consciousness and healing, but first, in building our foundation initially, know that the instant a photon of light transforms into mass, **it becomes two complementary and oppositely charged particles of positive/attraction and negative/repulsion**. In fact, even inside a proton (the center of an atom that electrons orbit around) are even smaller subatomic particles called elementary particles, up and down quarks, and each of these quarks has an oppositely charged antiquark. (Hawking, *The Illustrated a Brief History in Time,* 86)

So why am I teaching you this? Why is this important?

It is important to understand from a nonemotional perspective that every level of existence in the physical world—from the micro to the macro, starting with elementary particles that form into subatomic particles, subatomic particles that form into atoms, atoms into molecules, molecules into macromolecules, macromolecules into organelles, organelles into cells, cells into tissue, tissue into organs, organs into organ systems, organ systems into a human, and a human into a thinking, feeling, and perceiving being—**that each level of mass in the physical dimension of time and space derives from light—which is comprised of a**

pair of complementary positive and negatively charged particles.

So how then does this relate to your consciousness and anxiety?

Although you cannot see your thoughts or your consciousness, that does not mean that your thoughts are not energy. We cannot see sound waves or the endless information circulating around the ethers of the World Wide Web, but we know this invisible information is made up of energy, which is how we are able to tune in to its frequency. Your consciousness is energy too, and this is how Demartini's research on energy links physics, physiology, psychology, and spirituality together. Because if everything in existence partly derives from this one source, and if you understand the fundamental properties of how this source operates in the physical dimension of time and space, you then have answers to mysteries within the seemingly separate fields and how they masterfully link together.

Therefore, the fundamental laws of physics tell us that every thought, perception, emotion, belief, and experience is a form of electromagnetic light existing between a pair of oppositely charged particles of positive/attraction and negative/repulsion. Which means your consciousness is also made up of light, and therefore, operates dualistically in a dualistic environment. **The crucial point I want you to understand is that these two forces are not good or bad, but are the two essential forces that together make up light and the existence of our physical world in the universe.** They are the sacred interwoven opposites of the Yin and the Yang.

Both Positive and Negative Charges Make Life on Earth Possible

First, I want to illustrate the idea that positive and negative forces are neither good nor bad, but rather are essential components of life as we know it; here are a few fundamental, non-emotional examples:

One of the reasons you can walk on the surface of the Earth and not fall through to its center is because the electromagnetism in your body is pushing and pulling against the electromagnetism of the Earth.

Sunlight exists due to thermonuclear fusion in which positive and negative charges play an essential role. "The universe would be a vastly different place if the properties of the matter and force particles were even moderately changed...Stars rely upon fusion between stable nuclei and would not form with such alterations to fundamental physics." (Greene, *The Elegant Universe,* 12-13) What this means in layman terms is that due to the balance of positive and negative charges in electromagnetism, as well as the properties of gravity and strong forces, we have stars like our sun that can burn stably and slowly for millions of years— making life on Earth possible.

Electromagnetic energy also plays a vital role in photosynthesis. When light from the sun is absorbed by a plant, the plant captures the electron in its chlorophyll molecule, initiating the elaborate and masterful process of photosynthesis—filling our planet with oxygen to breathe and food to eat.

Water molecules are held together by polarized bonds made up of two hydrogen atoms and one oxygen atom that then create negative and positive poles. These electrically charged poles form hydrogen bonds with trillions of other water molecules—creating oceans, rivers, rain, and a glass of water.

Why am I sharing these scientific examples with you when this is a book on anxiety?

Because I want your mind to *get this*—I want you to be able to step outside your emotionally-charged story for a moment, and look at energy and consciousness from a practical, scientific, and universal perspective. In these four simple examples, you can see that attraction and repulsion are ESSENTIAL to life as we know it; we would not be able to live on Earth, nor have the basic necessities of life—sunlight, air, or water without them. Life in the physical world must have both positive and negative charges; neither one is better than the other, nor good or bad, but both are *equally* necessary for life.

So now let's tie this into your human experience

The 50 trillion cells that make up your body have evolved over millions of years through Earth's vibrational landscape of attraction and repulsion; **therefore, your senses evolved to measure an experience as something that you are attracted to or repelled by—*but not both simultaneously*.** For example, if you jump into the ocean in the middle of winter, your mind-body will measure that light experience as *'freezing'* and alert you to get the heck out of there!

Moreover, do you remember the first time you saw someone in a crowd that you were immediately 'attracted' to? And when you met that person, sparks flew, and soon your physiology literally took over and you wanted to be near that person no matter what, as though a force greater than you was drawing you to him/her? Or do you remember the last time someone rubbed you the wrong way, you found his/her demeanor completely off-putting, and you hightailed it out of there?

Your senses measure a situation and alert you if something appears safe and beneficial for your survival (representing the positive charge that you are attracted towards—that we can label as *supportive*), or your senses tell you when something is a threat to your survival (representing the negative charge that repels you away—that we can label as *challenging*). For instance, if your partner comes home and gives you a hug and tells you how brilliant you are and that you are unbelievably sexy, you would probably measure that light experience as *supportive*, and you would be *attracted* and want to draw your partner close to you (you might even feel so attracted that you would make-out, or snog as the Brits like to call it ☺). On the other hand, if your partner comes home and tells you that you smell, are lazy, and utterly boring, you would most likely measure that light experience as *challenging*; you would feel *repelled*, and (perhaps after flipping him/her the bird) you'd probably want to physically create distance between you and your partner (and you would most likely be uninspired to start snogging ☹).

Throughout your life, you have experienced your senses drawing you toward and away from things over and over again, but what you might not know is that your cells respond in the same way. *"When I was cloning human endothelial cells, they* retreated *from toxins that I introduced into the culture dish, just as humans retreat from mountain lions and muggers in dark alleys. They also* gravitated *to nutrients, just as humans gravitate to breakfast, lunch, dinner, and love. These opposing movements define the two basic cellular responses to environmental stimuli. Gravitating* to *a life-sustaining signal,*

147

such as nutrients, characterizes a growth response; moving away *from threatening signals, such as toxins, characterizes a protection response."* (Lipton, *The Biology of Belief,* 115)

Furthermore, our biology teaches us that like our senses, our cells cannot respond to an environmental stimulus by perceiving both sides of light simultaneously. *"My research at Stanford showed that these growth/protection behaviors are also essential for the survival of multicellular organisms such as humans. But there is a catch to these opposing survival mechanisms that have evolved over billions of years. It turns out that the mechanisms that support growth and protection cannot operate optimally at the same time. In other words, cells cannot simultaneously move forward and backward. The human blood vessel cells I studied at Stanford exhibited one microscopic anatomy for providing nutrition and a completely different microscopic anatomy for providing a protection response. What they couldn't do was exhibit both configurations at the same time."* (Lipton, *Biology of Belief,* 115-116, et al, 1991)

This teaches us two things. First, it reveals that when you are anxious, your body goes into a 'protective' response and you are unable to heal or 'grow' at the same time you are under stress. Secondly, it teaches us that human beings, which are multicellular organisms, have evolved to be dualistic in a dualistic universe, and measure the environment as safe or harmful, supportive or challenging, kind or cruel, but not both at the same time. **Yet, if we study the fundamental laws of energy, we know that this is actually an illusion played out upon us by our senses.** Both attraction and repulsion exist simultaneously—for they are ONE inseparable unit of light; however, we are unable to experience both sides at the same time because our senses, as Lipton describes, cannot move

148

forward and backward simultaneously. This paradox is what the ancient Hindu teachings referred to as 'Maya,' the physical world of illusion.

Now if we climb further up the ladder of understanding, your cellular biology builds into sensory organs, which make it possible for you to experience life through your physical body. This means that through your body, your senses and consciousness will immediately measure your experience of the world as either supportive or challenging—quite simply you'll move toward what you perceive supports your well-being, and away from what you perceive challenges your well-being. Make sense?

For instance, let's say you found out your partner cheated on you. Initially, you would most likely judge this painful experience to be extremely challenging and you might say:

- "Get away from me!"
- "Don't touch me."
- "You are such an asshole!" (Representing the side of a person that stinks, that you don't want anything to do with, versus calling your partner sweetie or honey, representing your biological desire to bring your partner close to your mouth).
- You might also shout…"Leave me alone!"
- "I never want to see you again!"
- "Get out of my sight - you make me sick!"

It is pretty clear to see, this type of language is highly charged, and represents a consciousness that measured this light experience as challenging and utterly repulsive. However, even though your biology and perception measures an event to be challenging, this is actually a lie or only a half-truth because light exists as equally challenging and supportive. Fundamentally, you cannot be challenged without equally being supported and vice versa.

Now, before I lose you by the jump we just made, let's take a look right now so I can show you exactly what I mean. What could be some positive, beneficial, and life *supporting* aspects to being cheated on? Perhaps...

- The person you were with actually did not treat you well at all, and being with him/her was in truth a rollercoaster of endless stress and drama, causing your health, finances, friendships, and career to suffer massively.
- Needing to constantly try and make your partner happy, you completely got sidetracked from your own goals in life.
- After separating, you rediscovered and reconnected with your true self.
- After separating, you were inspired to get back in shape and change your life.
- No longer having to juggle the emotions and drama of someone else all of the time, you now had tons of new available energy to focus on your career and finances, which coincidently began taking off shortly after you broke up.
- As painful as it was to lose the person that you loved, it was equally amazing to get your life back, get in shape, discover yourself again, feel lighter mentally and emotionally, get closer to your friends and family, have newfound freedom, and put more focus into your career and future.
- You gained invaluable insights as to what did not work in your relationship and intend to use this wisdom to be healthier for your next partnership.

- In hindsight, a few years later, you are actually incredibly grateful it all happened the way it did because you are no longer attracted to your ex anymore, and if it hadn't happened, you wouldn't have met your future partner with whom you are infinitely more compatible.

Hindsight is 20/20. It gives you clear vision of what *actually* happened from a wiser, grander perspective. In this example, we can see being cheated on wasn't just awful and wrong; rather, it was equally a blessing in disguise.

What if science could help us grasp a higher strategy for handling our sensitive human hearts, thoughts, and emotions? What if there are ways for us to speed up our learning process to see the hidden blessings and resolve our stress faster?

New research has shown that stress is linked to six leading causes of death; therefore, it is quite clear we require healthier, more effective means of processing our stress better, which is why I am hoping you will reflect on what I am presenting. For if the laws of nature reveal that we cannot have a positive without a negative, then how can we start using this basic understanding of light and apply it to our own lives? And instead of waiting years to see how a challenge equally served us, what if there was a way to speed up our learning and simultaneously resolve our stress and anxiety to have what Demartini describes as, "The wisdom of the ages without the aging process."

You may not readily see how you are equally supported during a challenge, but that *does not mean the support and benefit are not there*; in fact, the laws of nature tell us support *must* be there. This is where you may want to say, "No—this is too big of a leap. My model of the world and reality doesn't work like that—you can't personify physics into human experience."

If this is coming up for you, keep in mind you are not a physical being. You are an energy being. You appear as physical, but again this is an illusion played on you by your senses. In truth, you are made up of atoms and atoms are mostly made up of space. What your human eye sees is not the complete story; on the electromagnetic spectrum of light, the visual spectrum that humans are able to tune in and see is only a minute fraction of what actually exists. "Visible light opens such a narrow window on our universe that we are practically blind to its wonders. We might as well try to drive on the highway with a windshield painted black except for a half-inch slit in the middle." (Tyson, *One Universe at Home in the Cosmos,* 120) The truth is that you are not solid—that is an illusion. The world does not actually exist only as your human senses reveal it to you—there is a great deal more going on than meets the eye. You are a being of light made up of electromagnetic energy, and your consciousness is also frequencies of electromagnetic light. Therefore, your senses evolved to be dualistic in a dualistic environment, which means that when light energy transforms into mass as a pair of complementary charged particles of attraction and repulsion, you will either be consciously and biologically drawn towards what **supports** your survival, or you will be consciously and biologically repelled away from what **challenges** your survival. And from the moment you perceive an event to be more negative than positive, you are in bondage to that charge, and ruled by your emotions. Moreover, your highly 'charged' emotions and corresponding thoughts are energy particles and anti-particles that carry time, weight, charge and mass; therefore, your charged perceptions will run you, take up time and space in your mind, and actually cause you to feel heavier. Quite literally this means (as I am sure you have experienced thousands of times throughout your life), when you are upset about something or someone, your charged perception will literally *take you over*, creating tension and stress in your mind and body, as you mentally stew for hours, days, months, and even years. Know that if you continue to only perceive an event as more negative than positive, you will continue to be run by your emotional, one-sided perception, and your inner charge will continue to take up time and space in your mind, physically weighing you down, accelerating your aging process, and leading to symptoms in your body.

The transformative power of the Demartini Method occurs when your mind is able to see that both challenge and support are happening (and have happened) simultaneously in your life. Instead of coping with chronic daily stress and living inside a mind that reacts like a bouncing ball between the two forces of attraction and repulsion (aka emotional hangovers), you can learn to see both sides of life in balance and be more centered, present, and powerful...rather than being burnt-out, anxious, and overwhelmed. However, you cannot stay in perfect mental and emotional balance every moment because you live in an ever-changing, dualistic universe; yet, you can learn to surf between the two forces and find the sweet spot by practicing the art of balanced thinking and learning to ask yourself the questions that bring you back to center when the highs and lows of life *do* happen. Learning to balance your perception amidst challenges takes practice and consistent application, yet the moment you stop living in the *'effect' side* of life, and switch to consciously living in the driver's seat, your health, relationships, family life, career, and finances will reward you with an exponential return of health and empowerment in all areas of your life—as well as helping you to resolve your anxiety from the inside out. It truly is an invaluable tool to have at your disposal...in a world with a fair bit of challenge.

Do you know anyone who doesn't experience pain or stress in their lives?

Do you anyone who is 100% stress free?

The Dalai Lama, who is an internationally renowned teacher dedicating his life to the lessons of love, compassion, peace and happiness...*even he cannot escape pain and challenge*. Since 1959, the Dalai Lama has lived in exile, along with an estimated 150,000 Tibetans that look to him to guide them and to preserve their culture, national identity, and spiritual teachings. I imagine at times this must be quite challenging...but is this hardship entirely bad? Would the whole world even know the Dalai Lama existed if it *weren't* for his challenging circumstance? Because of his country's plight, he was turned into a global figure and launched onto the world stage, blessing him with a platform to share his spiritual teachings with millions of people around the world. The Dalai Lama used this great adversity to help him fulfill his greater potential and be a spiritual leader in the world. So even though he experiences hardship, it doesn't mean that it is bad, or that he is doing something wrong.

What if the next crest for human evolution and health is to use pain, symptoms, and stress as forces for good, and learn to embrace both sides of light—both support and challenge? What if within *every* pain there is actually a higher potential purpose? What if instead of coping with ongoing suffering and stress for years, you could learn how to use your anxiety as a source for tremendous good to change your life in deeply meaningful and inspiring ways...that not only help you to change your life, but also resolve your anxiety along with it?

Pain + Soul Purpose

What I witness again and again with my clients is that the very thing that challenged them the most (often with origins from childhood), is, in fact, 100% connected to what they love the most in life.

Why?

Because your pain runs deep. It runs all the way through you and into the very heart of who you are—therefore, it is a definite *driver* in your life, whether you are aware of it or not. Your pain wakes you up and gets your attention and sets you on your path to heal it, master it, and rise and grow within yourself to overcome it. For with every action there is an equal and opposite reaction—meaning that the bigger your pain, the bigger the hidden blessing will be.

The Demartini Method was created for this purpose: it is a powerful method to help you see both sides of light and to awaken your consciousness to your wisdom and the higher potential purpose that is *waiting to be fulfilled by you*.

The power of what I am presenting is something that you have to *experience* for yourself to *know* it to be true. Yet, you can gain invaluable insight and wisdom from hearing others' experiences. As this book is designed to share new knowledge and understanding with you, I asked two of my clients to share their self-healing journey with you in hopes that it will help you see what is possible when you balance your perception and embrace both sides of support and challenge in your own life. Fortunately, they were gracious enough to share their stories:

Growing up with Alcoholism

"Growing up in a household with two alcoholic parents was difficult. Our house was either Heaven or Hell; sometimes my parents were happy and in love and sometimes they didn't speak, for months or even years. They never fought and so I didn't know why they weren't talking. All I knew is that there would be some period of time when I would get stuck in between them as their messenger. 'Debbie, tell your father I need money for groceries." "Debbie, tell your mother there is a phone call for her." "Debbie, tell your father he has a doctor's appointment today."...and so on, until one day they would start talking again. The randomness and stress of not knowing when it would be Heaven or when it would be Hell was very hard for me as a small child to understand. At about the age of eight, I recall distinctly deciding that it was my responsibility to fix things. But no matter how hard I tried, there still ended up being periods of Hell, and each time it happened, I cemented the belief that if only I was better, it wouldn't happen again. This led to some significant depression as a teenager and young adult and an extreme fear of being in relationships.

"Over the years, I did work to identify the issues in my life that caused my depression and fear of relationships. Most of the work was around understanding the cause and learning to forgive. Although forgiving my parents was profoundly healing, it didn't relieve the pain or change my patterns of thinking. It wasn't until I worked with Bella and learned the Demartini Method that I realized that my pain has prepared me well for my life's purpose.

"Because I decided it was my responsibility to take care of my mom, I didn't go out much as a teenager. This left lots of time to study, and I learned to love learning and got very good grades in school. Not being home made me feel guilty and anxious unless I was doing something productive, so I got jobs at very young ages and started earning money and supporting myself. As a result of my good grades and savings, I was able to get into college and pay for it myself with little help from my family. The youngest of three, I was the first one to attend college in the history of our family.

"In an effort to try to understand the triggers of my parents, I became hyperaware of their moods and emotions. As an adult in the professional world, my keen ability to read people has made me a great team player and successful sales person. Today, I am a perennial top performer at the largest domestic bank in the U.S. and have been a perennial top performer in the country. So far this year, I am number one in sales not just in my region but in the entire bank.

"Often my parents seemed desperately sad and hopeless, and I wanted so badly to make that go away. My desire to fix things has given me an insatiable curiosity and yearning to find solutions. Searching for answers has led me to a new connection with my mind, body, and spirit. Through exercise, nutrition, and the healing arts, I have seen profound healing of individuals and their families. This quest for answers led me to my inspired purpose, which is to use my mastery in business and finance to create wellness centers that bring a variety of healing methods to a population that does not currently know they exist. By creating wellness-fitness centers that bring all of these healing tools together in one place, people can become aware of the healing arts and choose the ones that work for them and create their path to a fulfilled and healthy life.

"Seeing the pain my parents caused each other and our family, I became very much afraid of being in a relationship. As a child, I remember praying to God with all of my heart to never let me be dependent on a man. This fear of relationships *prevented me from getting into any type of long-term relationship, which was good because I did become independent, self-sufficient, and successful. Had I fallen in love as a young adult, I would likely have molded myself into being the person HE wanted me to be rather than avidly seeking the healing that I found. At the age of forty-four, I can proudly say that I have become the person that I would like to have as a partner. And as a result, I am now in a long-term relationship with a man that I can be fearlessly open and loving with, and this is the greatest blessing I could have imagined."*

If I had to write an essay on this, the title would be: The Gift of a New Way of Thinking

"From the Demartini Method, I got out of my own head and into my life. Life has its twists and turns and it teaches me all the time about me and others, but before I was living as a prisoner, trapped in my head. This method freed me. Things happen to me now and it's not 'here we go again or woe is me'...It's like this is a puzzle I've got to figure it out ... 'What is the lesson, where is the gift?'...I'm actually excited for the next thing to happen to me."

"Bella and I looked at the past and we really cleaned it up! I am now grateful for those hard times and the crazy people who have come across my path. They were my teachers. I found my freedom and purpose. I found myself, my talents, strengths, quirks, and gifts. And those gifts came from my childhood and the people who I used to think only let me down and hurt me and abused me.

"Honest & Maintain Confidentiality

"I grew up in an environment where there was a lot of manipulation and game playing, which as a child and for most of my adult life I felt I was the victim of. I didn't understand for a long time you can't win with such people, but I did everything I could in the pursuit of their love and approval, which proved to be elusive. I discovered that this gave me a desire to be a very honest, straightforward person. Keeping someone's confidence is important to me and I don't like to play games.

"Funny & intuitive

"When you live with violent and volatile people, you need to come up with strategies quickly to survive and stay on their 'right side.' Mine was to be the household comic and try to preempt what was inevitably going to hit the fan by using my intuition. What way is Mum looking? Is it going to be a good or a bad day? What can I do to fix her mood or change her mood? As an adult, now I am a master at making myself and everyone else laugh. I can break the tension with it. It really is the best medicine. People love to be around me and they feel better because of my hilarious sense of humor. I also use my special power of super intuition—you don't need to spell it out for me about how you're feeling. I will feel it and let you know it's okay...you're going to be okay.

"Listening, motivating and inspiring

"When I was growing up amongst the violence and abuse, I felt no one would listen to me and that I had nowhere to go with it all. Some of the abuse was sexual and the perpetrator

160

did a good job of making me believe the exit routes were all cut off to me. I work with students and young people now. All these qualities of mine change their lives for the better and they think that their Miss is pretty cool and so do I! It's made me listen to my students, really listen, to what they are saying, and to what they are not saying. I have the ability now of knowing what to say and what they need to hear to help move them forward. I make sure my students realize their own worth and that they move and take action.

"From this method, I have learned to be free from the baggage of the past, and most importantly, to not believe that just because I think or feel something is bad at first, the truth is that there is nothing bad...there are only teachers. There are no prisons only the limits we put on ourselves.

"These are the qualities that were gifted to me. Like all diamonds, they were formed in high-pressure environments. And like all diamonds, they and I are unbreakable."

7

Turning Darkness into Light

"When a particle collides with its antiparticle, they annihilate, leaving only energy."

~ Stephen Hawking

What if you could annihilate your emotional stress back into light? What if instead of feeling anxious and emotionally stressed out, you could more frequently embody a state of lightness, presence, wisdom, love, and gratitude?

When individuals balance their perception and *tune in* to both sides of light, across the board—it does not matter gender, nationality, or spiritual beliefs—they describe a feeling of centered presence brought about through wisdom, gratitude, and love.

Which brings us to the philosophical question: What is light? Is it love? Is there a wise intelligence permeating the universe?

162

Individuals who have had near-death experiences speak of a magnificent, radiant light that engulfed and filled them with a magnitude of love so profound that it changed their lives forever. Many also describe that within these experiences, time ceased to exist and there was a sense of oneness and a telepathic knowing or connection to an infinite, divine wisdom. Other spiritual light experiences are described by meditators when they attune with universal consciousness and have the experience of being bathed with blissful light, held in a timeless presence of unconditional, divine love. Various forms of self-healing methodologies can also create this powerful, transcendental state.

Coincidentally, in the quest to understand light, physicists inadvertently revealed that light mirrors many of these metaphysical descriptions. Light, intrinsically dualistic in nature, sometimes acts like a wave and sometimes acts as a particle. When light is in its infinite wave state, it travels at the speed of light (being timeless), it exists in multiple places simultaneously (an omnipresent, all-pervading unity), and can pop into physical existence, manifesting into *any* form (omniscient—having the inherent wisdom of all life contained within it.) When light exists as a wave in the formless dimension, we can see that this description in physics parallels spiritual light experiences; and when light exists as a particle in the world of form, the quality of energy is very different and exists in the dimension of time, weight, charge, and mass as kinetic energy in motion: e-motion.

Through Demartini's extensive research and working with thousands of individuals from around the world, his studies continually come back to **Light *being* Love**. He postulates that love in a wave-state has no separation, time, or mass, and it is in an unconditional, infinite state; however, when love is in a particle and antiparticle state, it exists in a conditioned, finite state of duality through the forces of challenge and support—and we require both sides of love in order to survive, thrive, and evolve.

*"Right in the middle between positive and negative emotions, between like and dislike, is the core of human experience, and it is nothing other than **love**...It takes both positive and negative particles in perfect synthesis to create light, and in exactly the same way, you need both sides of every event to hone you in on your true nature, which is also light. The light in the center is unconditional love; the emotional or particle waves are conditional love. They draw in their opposite side, which you need to bring you back to the center, but it's all love."*

(Demartini, *The Breakthrough Experience*, 31-32)

Love and Anxiety

The most profound medicine I have experienced is love. Love has the power to transform any hurt or resentment into a state of transcendent grace. It is, I believe, the most powerful force human beings can experience. Love is the medicine of your heart and Soul. Love is the power you can use to resolve your anxiety. Love is the elixir to heal and change your life.

But how can pain and darkness be in love?

Spiritual teachings will reference that love is all there is; yet, when a big challenge arises that seems utterly cruel and meaningless, it can be incredibly difficult for the human mind and heart to find love in such pain. So how can you find the inherent purpose within your greatest wounds? This is where the Demartini Method helps my clients and thousands around the world go beyond the appearance of meaningless cruelty—for you cannot change what has happened, but you can choose to learn and grow from what has happened and turn your adversities into your greatest strengths. You can either *choose* to make your pain personal, or you can *choose* to make your pain **purposeful**. If you choose to make your pain purposeful, you will have the opportunity to empower your life, be free from your past, and resolve your anxiety by transforming your *'suffering into a creative force,'* as Martin Luther King once eloquently stated.

When I work with my clients, I use many practical examples to help open up their minds to understand how their greatest challenges pushed them to grow and evolve in profound ways. In lieu of being able to have a direct dialogue with you about this, I will share several examples to demonstrate how Universal Love exists in challenge and struggle in ways that are not typically associated with our traditional view of 'love.' However, over the next few pages, I will seek to demonstrate what Demartini means when he says, "Love is the synthesis and synchronicity of complementary opposites. There is nothing but love— all else is illusion." When you see the higher purpose within challenges from a historical perspective, as we will look at now, I hope it will help you gain insight into the higher wisdom and purpose within your life. (For you are never given a challenge that you can't handle. If it is given to you—know that on a Soul level you are ready to learn from it, overcome it, embody it, and master it.) In addition, I hope these examples will help prepare you for the following chapter when you apply this work to resolve stress in your own life.

Love and Evolution

Between the 1500s and the 1800s, the life expectancy in Europe was just 30-40 years old. Humanity was trying to stay alive through harsh winters, failed crops, war, disease, childbirth, and childhood. Now millions can jump in their cars, drive to the grocery store, choose from food flown in from around the world, live in heated homes protected from the frigid elements, and have emergency surgeries, or C-sections if need be. Instead of surviving on minimal reserves of meat and potatoes during record-breaking freezing winters, in the 21st Century you can order in and have a movie marathon night on Netflix during a blizzard.

Yet, not that long ago, millions of people in the world lived under the dictatorship of brutal crown rule; freedom and democracy are human rights that were not easily earned. It was pain and oppression, not benevolence that empowered the masses to rise up, fight for their freedom, and establish a democratic consciousness on the planet. Similarly, African Americans empowered themselves against racial discrimination at the risk of being beaten, shot, or hanged, and it was certainly the pain of inequality that sustained the revolution through the hardest and scariest of times. Women, once regarded as second-class citizens in many countries, were also oppressed and unable to vote. Yet, it was gender inequality, abuse, sexual harassment, and discrimination that *initiated* a social revolution and demand for equal rights; it was not the pleasure and comforts of being 'a lady' that rose women to the streets. Women's rights around the world are still pushing societies to evolve, and I can assure you that it is not the kindness or pleasure of female genital mutilation, sexual enslavement, and honor killings that are bringing about these changes. Great challenges, throughout the centuries, have forced **disempowered groups of people to rise up and claim their power**. Just as great challenges in our history catalyzed human innovation to master farming, invent electricity, have clean drinking water, develop medicine, invent global telecommunication systems, etc. And we are not done. As old problems are solved, new ones are birthed as the laws of nature, of 'love,' continue to challenge and support us to higher levels of consciousness, to become a more civilized Earth.

"It is by those who have suffered that the world is most advanced."

~ Fortune Cookie (I just opened while editing this section)

Why am I bringing up such uncomfortable references? How will this help you and your anxiety?

First, because I have no doubt that what is connected to your anxiety is deeply painful. Therefore, I want to offer you a perspective from brutal and challenging times in our global history, to help you gain insight into the interconnection between pain and purpose—and cause and effect—even amidst the most challenging circumstances, in hopes that this will open up your mind and heart to perceiving your challenges from a larger, purposeful perspective.

Second, in the next chapter you are going to do exercises to dissolve your stress by looking at how past and present challenges have equally served you in invaluable ways; however, after having worked with clients for years, the answer I typically get back when I ask how a challenging situation benefited them is, "There are no benefits." If I got paid a dollar for how many times I've heard that one! ☺ So know when you are applying this work in the next chapter and you find yourself up against a wall saying, "There are no benefits. It was only bad," you can refer yourself back to this chapter, to remind yourself that pain throughout the centuries has purposefully served humanity...and the same law of cause and effect, of growth and empowerment, applies to you in equal measure.

It is well worth quoting renowned psychiatrist and Holocaust survivor Viktor Frankl again: "In some ways, suffering ceases to be suffering at the moment it finds a meaning. What man needs is not the discharge of tension at any cost, but the call of a potential meaning waiting to be fulfilled by him."

What is the call of potential meaning waiting to be discovered by you within your anxiety?

Tough Love

By in large, we can logically accept that we need a *certain degree* of challenge to develop and mature. We know that if we shelter our children from ever experiencing pain and challenge, this will be a disservice to them in the long run. For example, if you give kids whatever they want, whenever they want it, do their homework for them, make them food and clean up after them, never expect them to help out with family chores, while giving them unlimited spending money, you can easily see how this 'niceness' would eventually lead to a soft, dependent, lazy, entitled, spoiled, juvenile-adult who is ill-prepared to deal with the many demands of life on his/her own. On the other hand, if you challenge kids with healthy boundaries, give them chores to learn how to take care of themselves, expect that they will study hard, set the expectation for them to get a job to learn the value of money and the responsibility of budgeting, you can see how this 'toughness' would foster a strong, self-confident, independent, mentally capable, and ready-to-tackle-life's-challenges kind of adult.

So is love really only when someone is being kind and caring, soft and gentle...even if this type of nurturing leads to a disempowered, incapable adult? Doesn't that actually seem kind of *cruel* in the long run? Yet, the current, new-age association of spiritual love is that it is *only* to be supportive, peaceful, compassionate, and nice. So does that mean being challenging, tough, and strict is *not love*—even when 'tough love' fosters empowerment, independence, and confidence in the long run?

Most can see this as common sense, so **please know that the laws of nature only ask you to dig a bit deeper to see how this law equally applies to your *greatest challenges*.**

For what if the force of energy that gives us life and created the sun, Earth, moon, rivers, and air *knows what is best for us* and gives *us what we need* (just like a wise parent knows what's best for their child)...even if the challenges we are given are brutally hard at times? Democracy wasn't birthed due to the humanity of the monarchy, it was birthed by the brutality of the monarchy—yet brutality certainly served a crucial purpose in waking up the masses to claim their individual human rights and freedom. Enslavement births freedom. Constriction births expansion. Oppression births empowerment. Crown rule births court rule. Suffering births wisdom.

It is easy to think that life shouldn't be so hard and that it is not fair, or that it is inhumane that love resides in opposites...but *imagine if our world actually was one-sided.* Imagine if we lived in a world full of *only* men or *only* women. If the Earth's temperature was at a constant state of freezing or *only* blisteringly hot—nothing in between to create a balance. What if we *only* had day and could *never* see or learn about the infinite universe? Imagine never lying on the beach under the sun and forever living in a world of darkness. Imagine having a family like the *Brady Bunch*...gee whiz, good golly, wouldn't that just be swell?

The truth is, duality births the great diversity and magnificence of LIFE. Love gives you both support and challenge because you *require* both in equal measure, whether you like it or not. Your job (if you are ready to no longer be a prisoner to your stress, anxiety, or depression) is to stop trying to live in a one-sided reality that does not exist, nor expect that you should be treated by others in a one-sided, kind and considerate way 24/7. Wanting people to only be nice, respectful, caring, and considerate to you all the time, throughout your whole life, will most certainly cause you to suffer tremendously. Your job is to consciously understand that pain and challenge serve you invaluably (even if it is brutally hard at times) and to learn how to have more fun (yes, fun) with life's challenges instead of being bulldozed over by them. If you can learn to embrace the dance between pain and pleasure and consciously use adversity to help you grow and empower yourself—you'll certainly have **more fun** navigating the challenging terrain of human life. Instead of being stuck in stress (which again studies have shown is linked to the six leading causes of death), you can enhance the quality of your life by asking, 'Why is this happening FOR me?' rather than disempoweringly saying, "Why is this happening *to* me!" Replace one word in your way of thinking, and you will watch your life change dramatically. Sometimes it only takes a micro-shift to massively change your life.

When you learn to appreciate this Universal Law and embrace the two forces of love, you have the opportunity to resolve your stress more quickly and effectively. You have the opportunity to flow with daily challenges with greater grace, power, presence, wisdom, and gratitude. And when you embrace both sides of love, you annihilate emotional charges back into light...attuning to the frequency and light of your eternal Soul:

"Do you know when you have the polarizations of the positrons and electrons, they have mass and charge? Do you know when they are emotionalized in that form, I call that 'mass consciousness' and when they are synthesized and they are massless, I call that 'master consciousness.' And mass consciousness is the ignorant consciousness. And it lives in the positive and negative, the good and the bad, the attraction and repulsion and everything around them on the outside runs them. And when they finally bring those into equilibrium in their perception, they have the Soul. And I say that wisdom is the light of the Soul, and the light of the Soul rules through inspired action."

(Demartini, *Transcription of Personifying the Quantum Theory*)

The reason I use the Demartini Method as the cornerstone of my practice is because it not only transforms your disempowered story into an empowering one, thereby helping you to resolve your anxiety and upgrade your limiting beliefs, it also gives you direct clues into your Soul's purpose. When you know what inspires you, you will, as Demartini describes, "embrace both pain and pleasure in the pursuit of what you love." Each day will be fulfilling when you are aligned with your Soul's calling; for, when you clean up your baggage of the past and transform past suffering into meaning, you awaken to a greater purpose waiting to be fulfilled by you, which in turn elevates your current and future problems to become more purposeful and less stressful. Instead of challenges being meaningless inconveniences, they now become stepping stones helping you to refine your thinking, strengthen your stamina, master your composure, and everything and anything else that requires your fine-tuning—not as punishment, but as *preparation*…to help you succeed. You might need to master and grow in areas you have yet to realize. But not to worry—your challenges synchronistically arise in your life and show you exactly what you need to improve next. Additionally, you are inevitably going to experience challenges in life, so you might as well consciously take on the challenges that help you master what you love.

Visionaries and leaders throughout the world readily embrace and take on great challenges that inspire them. Take for instance Richard Branson, a renegade entrepreneur, an air balloon adventurer, a commercial spaceship buccaneer, an international philanthropist, a self-made billionaire—he has said his achievements are directly tied to his love of challenge. "My biggest motivation? Just to keep challenging myself. I see life almost like one long university education that I never had—everyday I'm learning something new. My interest in life comes from setting huge, seemingly unachievable challenges and trying to rise above them."

In the book, *The Best Advice I Ever Got,* Katie Couric collaborated with hundreds of the world's most brilliant and successful businesswomen and men, actors, singers, professional athletes, journalists, leaders of nations, comedians, and entrepreneurs to each write a short essay sharing the best advice they ever got. This book is made of gold and throughout it, there are two repeating themes. The first is to understand the vital importance of discovering what you love most in life, what you are good at, what lights you up, what fills you with a sense of purpose when you do it, and then go about doing it at all costs—even when it seems improbable that you will succeed—for if you truly love it then you'll have the staying power to make it a reality. The second theme is to learn to embrace challenges and the pain of temporary failure, to learn and grow from the wisdom within mistakes and adversity, to fail up, and to keep going no matter what.

In essence, this book beautifully mirrors what Integrative Health is really about: learning, growing, and evolving through your pain, mistakes, and challenges, and discovering what your gifts, talents, and purpose are—and then getting on the path of doing what you love. The truth is, your anxiety is not bad, it is an opportunity—*it is a doorway*. The key is not to let your wounds and challenges hold you down, but rather to learn to let them sculpt you, strengthen you, and bring out the very best in you.

When I used the Demartini Method to transform my greatest challenges into higher meaning and purpose, everything in my life changed. Everything. Suddenly, my pain cleared away my story of the past and revealed to me a much more beautiful reality that opened my eyes, awakened my spirit, inspired my mind, fueled my inspiration and inner fortitude, and set me off on an authentic, rewarding quest in which I gave myself permission to do more than I ever dreamed I could do in my life. My twenty-year-old self would never have dreamed what I now dream possible for myself, and I know that when I am in my 90s, reflecting back on my life, I will have lived many lifetimes in one because **I learned how to integrate this Universal Law of Pain and Pleasure, and, most important, applied it every day to my life.** I share this humbly because it has not been a path made of only singing birds and rainbows; however, it is deeply rewarding, fun, fulfilling, and ever expanding. Growing up with a loved one who suffered set me on a quest to find solutions to human suffering; now I love what I do and it is not 'work' to me. It is my calling that connects me to individuals all around the world. It also inspired me to write my children's book, *The Butterfly Story,* to teach kids how to believe in themselves and to find the hidden purpose within challenge. Witnessing suffering as I was growing up also connected me deeply to horrible pain in the world, and I am inspired to find ways to contribute to solutions on a global scale in my lifetime. Is all of this bad? Do I sound depressed, bored, held back in fear, or resentful—or do I sound like I *know myself* and that I am aligned with what I love and am inspired to take definite action in what is important to me on a Soul level?

Until I learned how to use pain in my life in a healthy way, I was restless, unfulfilled, and constantly run by short-term pleasures. When I took the time to consciously see cause and effect in my life and discover that what I loved most was in fact birthed by the elements I was deeply challenged by, I was able to transform my hurt into authentic gratitude, and thereby set myself free to give back to the world that I love. And not to sound cliché, but seeing pictures of our Earth from space absolutely humbles me and brings tears to my eyes. We live on a rare, blue, radiant paradise teeming with life—amidst a desolate backdrop of space. It is a miracle and a privilege to live here and be alive. Learning to use the principles of embracing both sides of love, of pain and pleasure, has given me the ability to make a contribution to the Earth and humanity in ways that are important to me and were not possible before. Instead of feeling hopeless, afraid, overwhelmed, or wanting to complain about the intense challenges of the world, my energy now goes into working where *I can make* a meaningful contribution. I am no longer dispersing my energy in emotional charges, being held back by past pain, self-protection, self-righteousness, and fear. I now take on challenges that inspire me...for I know a Soul-level solution is waiting to be discovered, and when I find it, it will be far more rewarding than any temporary pleasure.

Please know that within your greatest challenge is also an equal gift directly connected to something that you love and value most in life, and when you consciously find the higher meaning within your pain, you empower yourself to answer your calling in life.

This is why I am taking the time to write this book. I want to help those who are suffering know that this is only one side of a much bigger story, and that within your symptoms is an invaluable gift, guiding you to your excellence, vitality, and inspiring purpose in life. When you can humble yourself and learn to ask the questions that balance your perception to see both sides of light, you will discover the 'super-meaning' hidden throughout your life and the greater purpose that is *waiting to be fulfilled by you*. When you awaken to this higher meaning, you will naturally resolve your stress and anxiety by loving and appreciating your life for exactly how it is and *what your life has been preparing you for all along*.

This is the potential of resolving your anxiety from the inside out—not to just make your symptoms go away, but to bring meaning to why you had them in the first place.

So I will ask you, as I ask my clients:

Do you want to be run by your pain of the past and be ruled by a wounded story that keeps you stuck, or are you

175

ready to learn how to turn your challenges into rungs on a ladder upon which you can climb?

To self-correct your anxiety, our course has been set toward your True North, which is your *excellence*—returning to the light, love, and truth of who *you really are.* This is where we are headed.

Nothing less will do. xo

8

Enough Talk – Now it's Your Turn

The fun can now begin! And by fun, I mean rewarding. And by rewarding, I mean awesome. Well, I guess that really depends upon you! The exercises within the following chapters will push and challenge you mentally, emotionally, and spiritually. If you are willing to work hard, you will glimpse a new depth of meaning, wisdom, and purpose in your life, and resolve trapped stress that is exacerbating your anxiety. This section will require your dedication, commitment, and hard work, but just know that if you take the time to push yourself and go deep, your effort will reward you tenfold.

Before we begin, I want to explain two elements.

First, because I do not know your personal story and exactly what track patterns you need to work on, I am going to give you an exercise with questions designed to dissolve an extremely prevalent theme I see with anxiety—unresolved fear and stress around rejection and failure. Over the years, I have yet to work with one client where these two issues did not come up.

Why is this theme so common?

Rejection and failure happens to us all, which is probably why there are times when 99.9% of the population struggles with the belief:

"I am not enough."

Even if you don't resonate with this on the surface, my experience has shown me that this belief seems to be universal, even if it is deeply unconscious, and it will have an effect on you to some degree, whether you are aware of it or not.

Secondly, because I am not talking to you one-on-one, it is wise to start you off with something that is:

1. A warm-up to give you a sense of the true power of balancing your perception and learning how painful experiences have equally served you.
2. A way to help you get into the flow of this type of thinking. There is a graceful ease I find in working with the track patterns of rejection and failure that support individuals to naturally see the hidden order and purpose.
3. It has a powerful self-healing effect that will greatly benefit you.
4. This an entry point that does not involve jumping straight into the deep end. Anxiety is often connected to highly stressful experiences from the past and because we are not working one-on-one, I don't want you to try this on your own with the most painful stuff first. In addition, I recommend that you work with a trained professional on your most acute stress, as doing

it on your own can prove very difficult, and if only completed halfway can be counterproductive.

5. This is a warm up to the Demartini Method. If you would like to learn more about the Demartini Method, I recommend reading Dr. John F. Demartini's book, The Breakthrough Experience. I have my clients read this book when they work with me. It is a good one.

6. Before you read it, though, I highly suggest you do the exercise in this chapter as well as Chapter 10 and finish reading this book first, as Demartini's book is not written for anxiety.

7. In the last chapter, I have you investigate the specific track patterns connected to your anxiety described in Chapter 2 of Frontal Fear, Powerless Conflict, and Intolerable Stress. Again, if it is possible for you to work with a trained professional, I would suggest this.

8. You can apply the Demartini Method or another healing modality to resolve your stress. In Chapter 11, I offer a list of suggestions of different modalities you can choose from.

9. If you would like to use the Demartini Method, you can read The Breakthrough Experience, work with a Demartini Method Facilitator, or work with me in my intensive programs.

10. Additionally, I will be running an online class of the Demartini Method that you might be interested in as well, and you can go to my website, www.belladodds.com for more information.

11. Lastly, in Chapter 10, I take you through an exercise to upgrade your limiting beliefs! This is a powerful way to hold the work you have done once you have cleared out the stress holding an old belief in place.

With all of that said…now we can get started!

Exercise 1: The Hidden Benefits and Purpose of Being Rejected

1. **Get a notebook or paper to work with.**
2. **Make a list in chronological order of your earliest memory up to the present of whenever you were rejected (including every memory you have ever had when you felt rejected by love interests, parents, peers, coaches, jobs, universities, etc.)**

Yes, this absolutely includes when your seven-year-old crush did not 'love' you back. Our earlier childhood rejections are actually quite significant because this is where the wounded emotion of feeling rejected **took root in you.** (And if you remember, it felt devastating at the time). Kids are dramatic and see events in highly polarized ways as either extremely good or extremely bad. Unbeknownst to you, these emotions can be recorded as significant and stay trapped in your nervous system and unconscious. In the Beliefs section, we talked about the track pattern your psyche can get stuck on and the beliefs that get created through repeated stressful events. When you got rejected hundreds of times throughout your life, this can cause you to *unconsciously* be run by the belief, 'There is something wrong with me,' or 'I am not good enough.' (Emotions that would mirror this might be anxiety, worry, self-doubt, etc.)

Now make a list in chronological order of every memory you have of when you experienced rejection.

Example:

1. Charles fourth grade
2. Stephanie birthday party
3. Fifth-grade teacher Mr. Ginger
4. Did not get invited to the senior prom
5. Got made fun of in history class
6. Didn't get accepted into the advanced art class
7. Teenage partner broke up with me
8. Didn't get into the university of my choice
9. Didn't get hired at the bank
10. Didn't get a promotion at work
11. Three-year partner broke up with me

Note: There should easily be *at least* 20-40 memories. The more rejections you are able to remember the better. It can be hard at first, but start from your earliest memories and move up to the present. The deeper you go with this exercise the more powerful it will be.

3. Now that you have your list, look at each one specifically and go back to that memory and ask:

How did being rejected by that person or group serve me?

I'll give you a humorous example of my own to show you what I mean.

In third grade, I had a pretty epic crush on a boy. I would spend hours making love letters in class, drawing huge red hearts that said, "I love you!" Needless to say, he didn't love me back. Now rejection is rejection is rejection; in a lot of respects, it feels the same when you are eight as it does when you are an adult. You still feel *the sting of it* and are sad about it.

So what were some benefits of being rejected by my eight-year-old crush? Well, let's see. What were we going to do, make out? Go on dates? Hit all the bases? Yeah, none of those things (thank God!). Looking back, I can certainly be grateful that nothing happened. Interestingly, a funny twist on this story is that he changed schools, and I didn't see him for ten years until we went to the same university. His college roommate happened to be a friend of mine, and one night I went to their doom room. When I walked into the room, I kid you not, every square inch of my good ol' crush's wall was covered—*covered*—with porn. And we are not talking beautiful naked women; we are talking hard-core porn with many pictures of just—*just*—vaginas cut out...*all over the walls*. Ah, yeah. You know, it seemed more than a *little* over the top and all I have to say about that is ...thank God he never liked me back! Definitely didn't know this when I was eight, but he really wasn't the guy for me!

It is often quite humorous to see the benefits of your childhood examples of rejection, while your later teenage years and adult rejections become more significant and profound.

Note: If you get stuck, I have provided you questions to help open up your wisdom and intuition. Keep asking the question of 'how did this benefit me' until you are 100% grateful and wouldn't have wanted to change it in anyway. The test to see if you truly balanced your perception is to ask yourself, 'If I could still change this and make it happen the way I wanted to before, would I?' If you would go back and change any time you have been rejected, then you haven't completely awakened to all of the hidden gems and you need to look for more benefits. They are there. I promise you! On

182

the other hand, if you can see that every time you were rejected, it equally and profoundly served you, then you have truly completed the exercise and you will feel lighter, more present, and be one step closer to resolving your anxiety. Congratulations!

Questions to prompt your intuition to see the supportive, beneficial side in your childhood rejections:

- How was it a benefit that your childhood crush did not like you back? What would the drawback be if your crush did like you back?
- How did it help preserve your childhood innocence a bit longer, foster independence, and delay dating, codependency, drama, and distraction?
- How did it help you become closer to your childhood friends?
- How did being rejected by your peers help you grow as a person?
- How is it a benefit that you didn't hang out with a certain crowd that rejected you? How might you have changed as a person or gotten into trouble or acted in a way that wasn't aligned with who you really were if you had been friends with them?
- What would have been the drawback if your peers had accepted you into their group?

(Make sure you are answering these questions in full and not just reading them ☺)

- How did it serve you that a parent or a sibling rejected you?

- How did it serve you that a teacher rejected you?
- How did you not follow in an adult's footsteps?
- How did you carve your own path?
- How did you have inner drive to excel and make something of yourself?
- How did it push you to prove them wrong?
- How has it helped make you a successful person years later?
- How did you become more independent?
- How did your friends become your family?
- Are these friends still important to you now?
- What would have been the drawback if a parent, sibling, or adult figure had accepted you?

Tidbit: As I said before, I have worked with people for years. The first thing I hear is, 'There are no benefits' or 'I can only see a few, but that is it.' Keep in mind—**you are doing this for yourself!** You aren't doing it for anyone else, so if you want to feel strong, empowered, and confident, then channel that energy into working hard here. Keep going until you see how profoundly *every* rejection you had in childhood served you. Free yourself from unconscious chains of your past.

Questions to prompt your intuition to see the supportive, beneficial side in your adult rejections. (Answer these in chronological order—it helps your consciousness to see an underlying order and progression of purpose in the unfolding of time):

- How is it a benefit that you didn't marry that person? What would have been the drawback if you did marry him/her?
- How is it a benefit you were cheated on?

- How would your development have been stunted if you hadn't been rejected?
- How would you have compromised yourself or become someone you didn't want to be?
- How might you have given up your dream and played small for that person?
- How would you have stayed more juvenile and dependent?
- How would it have been if you actually stayed with that person for the rest of your life? Would you have grown restless, bored, or been stunted massively in some way?
- Are you grateful you didn't have children with that person in hindsight? What would the drawback have been if you did have children with him/her?
- When you got rejected, who did you meet later on that became a significant person in your life? How would your life be different if you hadn't met your new partner?

(Really...how did your rejections serve you? Reading these questions will not create light—answering them will! If you are in doubt that the other side is there, please go back and read Chapters 6 and 7 to get clarity and certainty. You do not exist outside of Universal Laws. Holding yourself back in an emotional wound for years is not serving you. Rise above your emotions to seek wisdom and dissolve your stress ☺)

- When your partner broke up or cheated on you, did you move to a different city? Did you get back in shape?
- Did an amazing job opportunity become available that you might not have taken because you were in a relationship and couldn't move to a new town?

- How did surviving heartbreak make you stronger and help you to know yourself better, love yourself more, and grow as a person?
- How are these attributes invaluable to you now?

(Empower your self-worth by awakening to a hidden gift stored within your unconscious. Go deep. Equal to the challenge is the hidden blessing...are you loving my book coaching ☺)

- How was rediscovering yourself and connecting back to your truth a life-changing, invaluable experience?
- How did it benefit you to get your life back on track? What would the drawbacks be if your partner had not broken up with you, and you got what you thought you'd wanted?
- Did your partner who rejected you become a person a few years later that you would never, *ever* want to date?
- Are you feeling rejected right now? How is it forcing you to become independent and strong, to rediscover yourself and get on track with what you really want in life?
- Could this person even give you what you really want, or are you wasting your precious time on a fantasy?

Note: Remember, go through EVERY memory you have and keep looking for the benefit and hidden support until you see the other side of light and are **100% certain** that each rejection served you profoundly. KEEP PUSHING YOURSELF TO SEE THE OTHER SIDE. This work is not easy, but it is well worth the reward. If you get stuck, you can ask, "How did it benefit me when he or she broke up with me: spiritually, mentally, emotionally, financially, vocationally, socially, physically? How did I get closer to my family?"

You will know you have completed the exercise because:

- You will feel present and poised
- Your mind will feel clear and calm
- You will actually feel lighter
- You will be grateful that each rejection happened *exactly* the way that it did and not want to change it even if you could
- Instead of having an emotional charge, you will feel grateful and in some cases laugh

Feeling any lighter and wiser yet? I hope so.

Exercise 2: The Hidden Benefits and Purpose within Your Failures

1. Write down a list of every memory you have of when you failed. This list can easily have 20-30 memories, and the more you remember and clear out the more power you will have access to. Write and number them individually in chronological order.
2. What were the hidden benefits and blessings when you failed?

Here is another quick personal example:

Growing up, you could say I was fairly uninspired by what I was learning in school. I can remember, starting to ask the question when I was seven years old, "*Why* do I need to learn this?" I really wanted to *know* the greater *significance* because getting good grades was not a motivation for me at all. It didn't mean that what I was learning *wasn't* significant— it just meant that I didn't see the importance. I had other things I would rather be doing. It wasn't until I got to university and I took my first philosophy class where all I got to do was ask the question *why* and reflect on the deeper, hidden meaning within everything that my love of learning got ignited. Once I left traditional school, I became a student of life and have been *highly* dedicated ever since. Now I would love to go back and take history, English, chemistry, physics, and geometry all over again.

Yet, the hidden blessing of not excelling in traditional schooling is that I moved toward a non-traditional path and way of thinking. Instead of thinking anxiety is a symptom that needs medication, my natural instinct is to research, explore, and understand *why* the body is developing symptoms and look for the underlying problem. If I had excelled in mainstream academia, I can easily see that I would have stayed within the groove because it would have been fun and I would have flourished; but because I didn't, I was pushed toward the path of my greater life's calling from an early age. (You were too—you just need to investigate!) The first eighteen years of my life of not excelling academically are serving the rest of my life to be aligned with what I deeply love. If I had been a straight-A student and thoroughly enjoyed reading *The Great Gatsby*, I know I would have chosen a different path for myself, because having to establish a new profession takes a deep inner drive and persistence to withstand the many challenges. Eighteen years of discomfort has prepared me with a great drive to persevere.

I was also a good athlete in gymnastics, dance, and soccer. My mom reminded me last year that when I was young, I had to do back handsprings and cartwheels when she quizzed me because that was the only way she could keep my attention. I did not pursue any of these sports to my full potential, and at the time, I felt like I wasn't good enough and wished I were better, but looking back now, it's easy to see the higher purpose. Had I pursued any of these sports to the highest level, that sport would have taken up *a lot* of my time, become my identity, and become my social network. Instead, I had freedom and flexibility to travel around the world and be a blank canvas in which to discover myself and my views of the world once I left home. If I had been as good in soccer or gymnastics as *I thought I wanted to be,* I certainly would have gotten a scholarship and pursued it well into university, maybe even beyond. Instead, my energy shifted to the international scale of humanity, healing, and the environment. I traveled to many third-world countries, driven by a deep desire to understand humanity from different life

189

experiences. Cambodia in particular impacted me. The people—and especially the children—left an indelible imprint on my consciousness. My experiences of traveling throughout my twenties to third-world countries exposed me to challenges and human beauty that still impact me to this day, inspiring me to find ways to be effective in my profession so that I may in turn empower women entrepreneurs in third-world countries so that they may in turn empower themselves, their families, and their communities. Equally, those experiences have helped me to not lose myself in the crazed, western world of short-term pleasures, or to be overly critical of myself trying to match current beauty trends, or to identify with 'material possessions' as who I am. Traveling humbled me. Seeing a man on the border crossing into Cambodia with burns covering his entire body, with his arms, legs, and eyes completely burned off, shifted my perception about pain and hardship for the rest of my life, making me humble, helping me to appreciate all that I am blessed to have, and awakening my ambition to want to help find solutions to suffering and massive problems on a global scale. These values will be with me for the rest of my life. In hindsight, it is a blessing that I was good at soccer—*just enough* to have fun with it—but that I was not good enough for it to have become my path, which was not in alignment with the rest of my life. (Nor was I the star for a few years of fame in a small pond that could have made the rest of my life seem less exciting. The real fun was yet to come.)

Now YOU look! But first, did you take ten to twenty minutes to write your list? If you haven't, STOP and do this now as this exercise is invaluable and doesn't work by doing it halfheartedly.

You also have equally profound and hidden blessings within your own life. Go back and look at *every* memory you have about failing and create a clear list. When you find one benefit and a domino effect opens up your intuition, follow this inspiring thread of insight. For instance, not being amazing at soccer led me to traveling a great deal in my twenties, but you can see if I had stopped there, how I would have missed a much bigger, more truthful story. Many fulfilling, life-changing experiences occurred because of my travels that still affect me to this day and are tied to my purpose. Allow your mind to see order, synchronicities, and interconnections in your perceived failures.

You can use the following questions as prompts to help open you up to your wisdom and intuition if you get stuck on specific memories where you failed and how these times served you invaluably:

- When you failed in school how did this serve you?
- Did it push you to work harder or find your own path?
- Did you get more into sports, art, or drama?
- Did you push yourself to overcome your failure and find a way to succeed?
- How did failing make you more social or improve your interpersonal skills?
- How did it push you in a different direction?
- If you had excelled and were the star, how would it have led you down a completely different path in life?
- How did 'the failure' help direct you toward what you really love?
- How did you take a 'failure' and turn it into a success? How did you FAIL UP?
- How did you grow stronger, more experienced, and wiser by overcoming temporary failure?

- How did you learn perseverance?
- When did it make you humble? How is humility a good thing?
- How would it be a drawback in your character if you never experienced failing?

(Are you answering these questions or just reading them? Reading won't connect you to the self-healing wisdom hidden within these perceived challenges. Find the truth and feel the reward of this powerful exercise. Now get to work, work, work ☺)

- How was it perfect that you didn't get the job you thought you wanted?
- What job did you get afterward? Who did you meet at the job that greatly benefited your life?
- What did you learn about yourself? What did you need to improve?
- How did losing your job help you get on track with what you really wanted in life?
- What would the drawback be if you hadn't lost your job?
- How was it essential that your relationship failed? How did you change your life afterward?
- How did failing in a relationship give you invaluable insights for who you wanted to be in your next relationship?
- How did it help teach you how to treat your next partner with more maturity?
- How did you empower yourself spiritually, mentally, emotionally, physically, financially, socially, and vocationally?

- How did it help you to become more humble and more centered?
- What would the drawback be if your relationship had not failed?
- How did failing slow you down to think things through more wisely?
- How did it help you to develop a plan?
- How did you learn the essential ingredients of success: patience and persistence?
- How did you grow closer to people while you were recovering from your temporary 'failure'?
- What essential things did you learn that were much more valuable in the long run than if you would have 'succeeded?' How would that 'success' have actually been a great disservice to you?
- How was that failure (temporary delay) essential in forcing you to see where you needed to mature, develop skills, and grow as a person in preparation for your eventual success?
- How did you not fail at all?
- **How have you never *really* failed?**

Good job! I know this took you some time, but it is amazing what a couple of hours of hard work can do to completely shift your perception that will serve you for a lifetime. If you went to the depth and pushed yourself to see both sides equally, this exercise will have cleared out a tremendous amount of repressed stress, worry, fear, and shame that has been holding you back, creating self-limitation, self-criticism, self-doubt, and contributing to your anxiety. To see the other side is to see ACTUALITY and to know that the truth is that you have never been 'not good enough'...but rather these were *necessary* events for your development so you could learn, mature, discover, refine, and go in the direction *right for you.* Some relationships were not meant to happen for sacred reasons; some job opportunities were not for your highest good; and in some cases, you had to be rejected by someone to meet the right person who would impact your life in ways you could not have previously imagined or known were even possible.

Exercise 3: Own Your Worth

"If you don't see your worth, you will devalue yourself and so will the world."

~ Demartini

Now that you have seen that those times when you were rejected or experienced temporary failure served you in meaningful ways, this greatly **helps your anxiety by decreasing the gripping fear of needing to be perfect, needing to control everything, or the fear of never messing up. Taking the time to do this exercise will have shown you that if you ever do 'mess up,' it is not only a one-sided negative event, but rather an equally meaningful *and* positive one.** Additionally, it will have helped you to realize that there really is no such thing as 'perfect' in the sense of excelling or getting what you want *every time,* but in fact your *imperfections* are the only true perfections. You are not supposed to get it right every time or get what you want every time because there exists a wisdom greater than yourself, giving you exactly what you *need* for your optimal growth. If you did this exercise to the depth, you will have undoubtedly proven this to yourself and perhaps humbly realized that the saying, "Things happen for a reason," isn't just a nice thought, but rather it is a profound and sacred truth.

For this next exercise, you need to look and own where you *are enough*...actually, you need to see where you are *awesome*!

Our biology and psyche often **maximizes the challenging sides** of reality while **minimizing supportive** and uplifting sides. For example, if you stopped to quickly grab a sandwich for lunch on your way to work and someone said to you while waiting in line, "I love your laugh! It is so uplifting!" you might smile and say, "Oh, thanks!" Then a few minutes later, you'd have bought your lunch and most likely would be thinking about the next thing that you needed to do...completely forgetting about the lovely, uplifting comment you just received. On the other hand, if someone in line made a snarky remark in a demeaning tone like, "Can you keep it down? Your laugh is obnoxious." There is a good chance that five to ten minutes later you would still be a bit perturbed and find it hard to fully concentrate because in the back of your mind you would still be thinking about how rude that asshole was. And the next time you laughed, you might even be a little self-conscious about what other people think of you.

Or your partner could tell you, "You look so sexy!" You might say "thanks," but still not totally believe him/her and minimize how great you do look. However, if your partner said, "Are you sure you want to wear that? It is makes you look a little wide." Yeah, how well would that go over? How many years later might you still *actually remember* that comment?

Why do challenges or criticisms stick so much more significantly in our memory than complements? I have noticed that we maximize challenge, while equally minimizing support. Perhaps it is because the negative charge has a counterclockwise spin that literally spirals in a downward direction and weighs you down, versus when you perceive something supportive, you measure that light experience as positive, which has a clockwise spin that spirals upward, making you feel uplifted and light. Whatever the case may be, challenging experiences tend to really stick in our memory and weigh us down, gripping us much more tightly than positive experiences. So let's combat some of this overemphasis on the negative, shall we?

Confidence and Self-Love – Own Your True Worth

This exercise is pushing you to see the truth, to not minimize your exceptional talents and gifts, and to OWN your worth.

1. Think of specific memories or events where your strengths and gifts helped you, others, and the world at large. Come up with a list of 100-200 memories and positive attributes. Here are questions to open up your intuition, but please don't feel limited to just this list. These are prompts to get you going and open up your mind and memory.
2. What are your strengths, natural gifts, and talents?

(List them now and remember you have as many strengths as you do weaknesses. Being human means you will have both equally.)

*   What do you love? What do you love doing?
*   What are you good at? What are you great at?
*   How do others greatly benefit from your gifts?
*   When have your strengths helped others?
*   What little things do you do that brighten people's day?
*   When do you make people laugh or smile?

(Answer these questions in full! You are not serving yourself or anyone by minimizing your worth. Somewhere *you know* where you are brilliant. Don't hold back or play small. You do that enough already ☺)

- When have you come to someone's aid?
- When did you do well in school and pass a test or get a high grade in a class? (List all you can remember. Don't minimize your victories.)
- When have you received positive recognition?
- When have you been committed to and completed a challenging task?
- When have you been told that you looked sexy?
- When have you been sought after by multiple people at once?
- When has someone declared his/her love to you?
- When has someone said thank you for being in his/her life?
- When has someone told you that you helped change his/her life?
- When have you been there for others and stuck by them while they were going through a hard time?
- When have you made people feel important?
- When have you been an amazing listener?
- When have you made people laugh or feel better?
- When have you gotten a raise or promotion?
- When did you get accepted into a program or university?
- How many times were you successfully hired for a job?
- Where do you shine as a parent?
- How have you profoundly touched the life/lives of your child/children in beautiful ways?

(Answer these questions. The deeper you go, the greater the reward will be!)

- When have you made your child/children feel special?
- When have you shined at work?
- List all the times you rocked it at work and received recognition.
- List all the times you made someone proud of you.
- List all the times you overcame great adversity.
- How many times have you been able to pay for all your bills month after month after month?
- When have you challenged someone, knowing it was for his/her highest good?
- When have you shown tough love that helped someone wake up and change his/her life?
- When have you been humble and admitted how you played a role in an argument and opened up the other person to communicate with you?
- When have you been a rock of strength in your life and for others?
- When did you overcome a monumentally hard task?
- When did you make the impossible work?
- When did being yourself make a huge difference in someone's life?
- How has your light impacted others and the world?

Answer these questions in full. This exercise is a powerful piece in self-healing your anxiety. Go to the depth and list *at least* 100 attributes of your gifts, as well as instances where you overcame challenges and shined brightly. If you truly want to own your worth, get to 200 and then keep a journal and add to it. You, your loved ones, and the world will greatly benefit if you stop minimizing yourself. A Microsoft study in

2008 found that there is 6.6 degrees of separation between you and everyone else in the world, and a more recent study in 2011 from the University of Milan showed that with Facebook, we are no more than 4.74 friends away from *every other person on the planet*. (John Markoff and Somini Sengupta, *New York Times,* November 21, 2011) Please stop underestimating and undervaluing yourself. Who you are does impact the world...creating a ripple of cause and effect throughout the magnificent web of life.

If you do this exercise to the depth and really take the time to look, see, and own your worth, you will *physically feel different*. To check the quality and depth of your effort ask yourself:

1. Do I feel empty or full?
2. Is my thinking scattered and worried, or calm, clear, and poised?
3. Do I see my place and value in the world more clearly?
4. Will feeling more confident and owning my worth help relieve some of my insecurities and anxiety?
5. How is owning my value as a human being going to help me feel worthy to take more action in my life, strengthen my confidence, and assist me to feel more fulfilled in my life?
6. How will I (and others) benefit when I stop playing small, stop minimizing myself, and take more inspired action?
7. How would I love to make an impact in the lives of those I love the most, and/or help to make a difference in the world in some way big or small?

9

The Healing Power of Love

There is a deep desire within us all to be loved, seen, heard, and appreciated for who we really are. Yet we often don't do this for ourselves. We do the opposite—we are *so* hard on ourselves. But if we don't love, see, hear, and appreciate ourselves, how can we ever *allow* others to fully love us? How can we fully allow amazing opportunities to come our way and allow ourselves to flourish without sabotaging ourselves on some level if we don't truly feel we are worthy of it deep down?

Every day I say, "I am made of love. I love myself." I say it when I feel centered, disconnected, peaceful, stressed, sad, inspired, lonely, etc. I have learned it is *essential* to be on my own side no matter what. Loving myself is an *essential* ingredient to my well-being. I am human. I will experience all the colors of what it is to be human. I have strengths, and I have weaknesses. Each day I will fail, and each day I will succeed, but no matter what, I am still worthy of love and worthy of being on my own side. During periods in my life where I didn't truly love and value myself, I paid the price. It was a very painful six years. I actually wasn't even consciously

200

aware of how hard I was being on myself, until one September afternoon, it came clear to me that I had gone far from my center. When I finally woke up and realized this—at that moment—I stopped what I was doing, I came into the present moment, put my hands on my heart and consciously said, "I am made of love. I am made of love. I am made of love. I love myself."

From that day, I began my inner journey back to self-reverence and unconditional love—even, and especially, when I felt like I was struggling. I have consciously continued to practice self-love and appreciation since that time, which includes this very moment as I am writing these words. Each day as I practice unconditional love for myself and others, this healing energy grows stronger within me. Love continues to reveal to me more beauty and strength that lies within my heart. I am tearing up writing this because learning to love myself and others unconditionally has opened my heart to a strength that I did not have access to before. The strength of unconditional love comes from an Infinite Source. By opening to this source day by day, I have greater patience, I see others more clearly, I see their pain and when they are acting out of protection, and I learn not to take their actions personally, rather to respond with deeper understanding, connecting to their heart and their true intentions. Now during periods of greater challenge, I have continued to consciously choose to open my heart instead of shutting down and protecting myself. Having weathered many difficult periods, I know that I do not need to shut down my heart, for it is much stronger than any pain. This has been one of the most profound blessings, and I am only just beginning to discover what it will mean for my life and how it allows me to be more authentic with others, which is why I am sharing something so personal with you. How might your life change if you actively seek to be on your own side every day and seek to come from the strength of your love, rather than your fear?

The Power of Love

Demartini has a story I want to share with you from his book, *The Breakthrough Experience*:

"A number of years ago, I had the opportunity to talk with a gentleman in a San Francisco hospital who was dying of AIDS. The doctors gave him just a couple of weeks to live. When I came into his room, he was emaciated, covered with sores, leaning over in bed, and propped up with pillows. I sat down next to him and grabbed his hands and wouldn't let go.
"I'd never met the man until that moment, but I just held his hands and looked him straight in the eye and said, 'No matter what you've done or not done, you're worthy of love.'
I had him repeat it over and over again until it finally penetrated his heart and he started to cry. He leaned over into my lap, and I put my hands on his back and kept saying, 'No matter what you've done, you're worthy of love,' while he cried and cried and cried.
"He finally lifted up his head a little bit and looked at me and said, 'That's the first time in my entire life I've ever thought that. That's the first time I've ever given myself permission to love myself.'
"In spite of the dire prognosis that man lived almost two more years."

I feel this story profoundly illustrates the simple, yet powerful and life-changing effect of loving yourself—no matter what. An autoimmune disease is literally when the body starts attacking itself. Perhaps what helped this man live almost two more years, despite having been on his deathbed, was the healing power of love, and loving himself for the first time in his life.

Love, without question, is an extraordinary force in the universe.

Can you flood your body with this healing power?

Do you feel you are worthy enough to fill your body with unconditional love?

Do you feel a resistance inside yourself? If so, I am curious, when will you ever *be enough* to fully love and accept yourself? When will you be good enough, have accomplished enough, earned enough, done enough, overcome enough, proved yourself worthy enough, or looked good enough to believe you are worthy of unconditional love?

Love is not dependent on societal success...love is who you are, *right now*. In this moment, you are love—you are made of stars, of light, of love. In your strengths and weaknesses, in your victories and failures, and in your praises and rejections—all of who you are right now is *enough* to put your hands over your heart and say, 'I am made of Love. I am made of Love. I am made of Love. I am Love. I love my Self.'

The Humility of Unconditional Love

Coming from the place of *I am love* and *I am enough* is not vain—it is actually a great act of humility.

A large tree with deep roots opens itself to receive the abundance of the sun, and in so doing gives a blessing to all the world with clean air, homes to thousands of creatures, shade from a hot summer day, all while meditatively swaying in the breeze, instilling a healing serenity upon the land. Imagine if the tree thought, "I am not enough." Imagine if the tree did not feel worthy to grow deep roots, or accept the full gifts from the sun. Imagine if it only grew half of its potential branches and made half of its leaves because it said, "I am not good enough or worthy enough to receive the blessings of the sun, and fully be myself." Imagine how we *all* would suffer if the tree held itself back from the light of its full magnificence.

The feelings and belief, "*I am not enough*" may on the surface feel as though you are being humble, but the truth is, *the deep truth is*, the feeling "*I am not enough*" is not being humble—it is actually being *selfish*. "I am not enough" derives from your fear and your perceived self-lack that acts like a powerful black hole inside your being, distorting your perception, consuming your light, and pulling you into a bottomless pit where you get stuck only being able to focus on *yourself*. From your fear and lack, you are afraid to take action because you are worried *you* will fail, or terrified of what others will think of *you*. From this black hole, you feel empty. From here, you are stuck in your suffering and are separate from the whole. From here, you are too afraid to be vulnerable and show the world who you *truly* are. From here, you are more focused on yourself and your perceived shortcomings than on focusing your attention on how you can be of service. From here, you must protect yourself and put on a show. From here, you are afraid to fully love others and be loved. From here, you cannot clearly see the path that leads you to where you want to go. From here, you don't feel worthy to have what you most desire. From here, you attack others and yourself. From here, you blame. From here, you justify. From here, you play small. From here, you cannot do what you would love to do because you do not feel capable or worthy to do so. From here, you are hurt that others do not see and appreciate you—but how can they when you do not see or appreciate yourself?

We can fear believing '*I am enough*' because we don't want to act vain, but the truth is that coming from '*I am enough*' is an act of great humility—a humility that stems from a wise and honest heart that bravely asks, "How may I serve?" Instead of hoping or wishing you could have what you want, your prayer may shift to, "Please give me strength to believe in myself, to have clarity of vision, stillness to hear, the ability to be patient and persevere, the confidence to be vulnerable, the presence to connect with my Soul, the courage to obey, and the certainty to take definite action and be a loving service to the world." From this humble place, your *enoughness* fills your body, heart, mind, and spirit with a confident call to definite action. From here, you are not focused on yourself or your perceived shortcomings—you are focused on your strength, what inspires you, and how you can serve others using the gifts you have graciously been *given*. From here, you can clearly see a path that will lead you to where you would love to go, and you have the courage to take action every day to make it a reality. From here, you put your energy into solving the problem. From here, failures are only temporary. From here, delays are essential stepping-stones to grow stronger and wiser so that you may fulfill your destiny. From here, you love yourself fully and are strong enough to be vulnerable. From here, you are honest. From here, you will be your Authentic Self *without apologizing for it.* From here, you embody your strengths and feel worthy to help others. From here, your vision is steadfast, true, and fixed on your definite purpose. From here, you will know your gifts and abilities are not for you alone, but were blessed upon you to be shared in service as a blessing for the world. From here, you will shine your light to the fullest and brightest of your potential, contributing to the world in the way that *only* you can. From here, you will manifest the magnificence of your eternal Soul.

"Our deepest fear is not that we are inadequate. Our deepest fear is that we are powerful beyond measure. It is our light, not our darkness that most frightens us. We ask ourselves, "Who am I to be brilliant, gorgeous, talented, and fabulous?" Actually, who are you not to be? You are a child of God. Your playing small does not serve the world. There is nothing enlightened about shrinking so that other people will not feel insecure around you. We are all meant to shine, as children do. We were born to make manifest the glory of God that is within us. It is not just in some of us; it is in everyone and as we let our own light shine, we unconsciously give others permission to do the same. As we are liberated from our own fear, our presence automatically liberates others."

~ Marianne Williamson

Whatever I have done, or have not done I am worthy of love.
I am made of Love. I am made of Love. I am made of Love. I am Love. I Love my Self.

"Use me, till you use me up."

~ Oprah

10

Upgrade Your Limiting Beliefs
Work with a Power a Million Times Greater than Your Conscious Mind

Limiting beliefs are infinitely easier to upgrade and change once you discover that they are *not even true!*

If you completed the exercises above, you should now be able to see with greater clarity that when you experienced failure and rejection, those wounding experiences were actually *not the entire story.* The truth is your failures and rejections led to awesome developments in your character that made you who you are today; they also likely changed the trajectory of your life's path profoundly in ways that you are now grateful for and wouldn't want to change—even if you could.

Going back and perceiving your life from the two sides of light—from both challenge *and* support—you tune into a greater wisdom of cause and effect in your life...and *change your story*.

When you change your story, your old beliefs suddenly don't match what *actually* happened, and are now outdated chains, **holding you back to a past that doesn't even exist.**

Seeing your story through the lens of wisdom and truth requires that you now create new, empowered beliefs to match your *new* understanding, and retrain your body and consciousness with empowered truth and wisdom. In doing this, you create a ripple effect from the core of who you are out into every aspect of your life. When you upgrade your beliefs, your thoughts mirror these changes. And when your thoughts change, your actions and responses to life change, and instead of being stuck in anxiety you are centered and strong. This dramatic shift will restore your physiology to equilibrium—resolving your symptoms from the inside out.

This is why I have taken the time to give you an **in-depth** understanding of the Integrative Health process. These separate puzzle pieces are not separate at all, but are unified, and when you bring them all together you create a comprehensive approach toward resolving your anxiety from the inside out by changing your story to one that is infused with wisdom, truth, purpose, love and power—upgraded from your old story that was once rooted in fear, self-doubt, and lack.

So let's get started!

It has been said that your subconscious and unconscious mind run 95-99% of your brain's processing power, which means that your conscious mind is only in control of about 1-5%. You do not consciously beat your heart, digest your food, or repair a cut, nor are you consciously overseeing every habitual action like speaking, riding a bike, eating, walking, or driving a car—many of your habits and behaviors don't take much thought, effort, or discipline, and you can go on auto-pilot, allowing the power of your subconscious mind to take over. Dr. Catherine F. Collautt, an expert in working with the subconscious mind, shares how there is a great opportunity in working with this aspect of yourself if you can learn how *to harness its power to work for you!* "By far our greatest processing powerhouse is our subconscious mind. Scientists will tell you that the power of the subconscious is perhaps a million times greater than the conscious mind, and the point of that is not to say that your ego and your will are weak, but to recognize that as powerful as they are, there exists an asset within us that is even more powerful."

Your subconscious is very much like a computer, and it runs on programs that you have given it such as:

I am not good enough.

You may not be consciously thinking this, but if your subconscious is running on a program of this inner child limitation, it can cause you to feel anxious, lack confidence, and second-guess yourself—all of which will intensify your anxiety. In the previous exercise, you dissolved your emotional fuel and stress attached to rejection and failure by discovering a higher purpose and opportunity hidden within these stressful events. In so doing, you simultaneously cleared the energy that can fuel the limiting belief of 'I am not enough.' However, this does not typically clear an acute belief completely, because Achilles Heel beliefs are programs that have been deeply embedded within your subconscious for decades, and it can be difficult to entirely transcend them unless you also work with the power of your subconscious mind.

Why?

Because at a million times more powerful than your conscious mind, it is pretty clear who is going to win! Fortunately, this also gives you an invaluable and favorable advantage, which is that you have a profound and powerful

**asset ready and capable to work in harmony with you 24/7—
if you upgrade your beliefs and give your subconscious mind
the right program.** To get your subconscious mind on board
with what you want and upgrade a limiting belief, it is your job
to make sure that you give it crystal clear and optimal
programs to run on 100% of the time—even when you aren't
consciously thinking about it. This requires that you regularly
debug, reprogram, and upgrade limiting beliefs as you
discover them so that your inner powerhouse can be your
most valuable asset. Or as Collautt describes it, "Your job as
president and CEO of yourself and your life is to get the most
out of this most dependable and capable employee (or friend)
that you will ever have at your disposal."

When you upgrade your program to *I Am Good Enough*,
you will begin to automatically tune in to opportunities that
before you would have unconsciously tuned out or
immediately thought weren't possible for you. You will say yes
instead of shrink and say no. You will also feel capable and
competent even if something is hard; you will enjoy the
aliveness and growth of a challenge, rather than feel flattened
and defeated by it. And your new belief of *I am enough* will
foster new habits, behaviors, and internal presence—all
preparing you for auspicious opportunities. You may naturally
crave healthier foods, feel more energized, be disciplined to
work out, as well as have healthier, more openhearted,
relationships. (Many arguments with loved ones can actually
derive from our own sense of not feeling good enough, and
we can shut down and protect ourselves, or get upset and
ardently defend this inner vulnerability.) When you believe
you are enough, you will automatically give yourself
permission to go after what inspires you and what you care
about most because you will have a great strength on board
with you—*your belief in yourself*. Now don't get me wrong—

you will still have challenges, and you will still have more levels to work through in self-healing your anxiety; however, you will be on your own side and have an inner congruency in your life, rather than wasting your energy fighting an internal battle of self-doubt and low self-worth.

Upgrade your beliefs with grace...skip the blood, sweat 'n' tears approach

Collautt offers a powerful and beautiful approach in working with the subconscious mind that is in perfect alignment with the theme of this book in that she believes there exists a more powerful source of wisdom to learn from and work with than our conscious mind alone. Within this book you have learned that limiting beliefs derive from stressful events, and now you have learned that during these stressful events, there were also hidden blessings helping to support you to grow in ways you did not see before (with every action there is an equal and opposite reaction); and through glimpsing this higher order of cause and effect, you have learned that rejection and failure served you simultaneously on an essential level. You have also looked at how you equally have succeeded and excelled in your life, providing further evidence to disprove the limiting belief *I am not enough*. And as Universal Laws permeate all levels**, there are also positive and valuable attributes within the negative belief *I am not enough*.**

Instead of trying to force your subconscious mind to change and upgrade to new beliefs by tirelessly telling yourself affirmations—"I am good enough, I am good enough, I am good enough" (which can easily feel monotonous and run the risk of making you feel that you are lying to yourself if you don't really yet believe it)—Collautt offers a simple process to work *with* your subconscious mind from an angle of reverence, trust, and gratitude that not only awakens you to the higher meaning and wisdom hidden within your temporary limiting beliefs, but simultaneously supports you to gracefully upgrade them, in lieu of struggling and forcing your subconscious mind to change. Her work opens the door to create a sacred relationship with your subconscious that enhances your intuition, allows you to love and trust yourself more, as well as discover more of who you truly are in your core essence.

Before we begin, I want to share that I am slightly tweaking the questioning because Collautt's exercise is set up to address the limiting beliefs and fears you have about getting what you want, such as inner-sabotage to becoming rich and successful. The questions are the same in essence, but we are going to come at it from a slightly different angle as this exercise relates to your anxiety.

Ready?

Exercise 4: Upgrade Your Limiting Beliefs with the Power of your Subconscious Mind

Step 1: Recognize Your Limiting Belief + Be Humble

1. What is your limiting belief? **(Right now we are working with *I am not enough.)***

(In the future, to uncover what belief is holding you back, go to the exercise in chapter 5 using either the Kinesthetic Exercise or the Mental Exercise to make your unconscious conscious and get clear on what belief you want to upgrade.)

2. Once you have identified your belief, you want to get humble, be open, and trust that your subconscious has something very important to tell you, because at a power a million times greater than your conscious mind, it most certainly does.

Summary: Identify your limiting belief. Get humble, reverent, and curious.

Step 2: Get Specific + Find Purpose

1. Humbly ask your subconscious *why* it is holding onto this belief for you. How is your subconscious mind actually looking out for your best interest?
Such as: What strengths, skills, ethics, values, and abilities have been sculpted within your character *because* of this limiting belief? How is this limiting belief helping you to actually *be true to yourself*? What Soul Values is your subconscious looking out for to make sure that you are embodying the core values necessary for your success?

Not feeling good enough could have pushed you to have a great work ethic, to go above and beyond, or have high goals in your life. (Unconsciously, this can come from a perceived void within yourself of not feeling good enough, which drives you to accomplish great things.) Not feeling good enough might have fostered a desire to want to connect with others on a genuine, carrying, and humble level. **The higher intention of your subconscious mind works on behalf of your Soul Values, not your ego.**

Now you investigate. Converse with your subconscious as you would a dear friend by coming from a place of genuine curiosity, respect, and a desire to understand. Ask your subconscious *why* it is purposefully holding onto this negative belief *for you*. What is the higher intention and gift within this belief? You'll want to hear your subconscious's case because it has *priceless wisdom* to share with you.

Come up with 20+ benefits in the seven areas of life— Spiritual, Mental, Emotional, Vocational, Financial, Social, Familial, and Physical—to see how this 'limiting' belief is actually propelling you forward and **keeping you on track with your true core values**. Keep asking until you see with 100% certainty how this belief actually has helped to instill sacred qualities in your character that are invaluable, and/or has helped to show you the core of who you are and who you wish to continue to be.

Summary: How is this belief helping you to be the person you really want to be in the world?

Step 3: Make a Promise

Make your limiting belief a non-issue by making a promise. Collautt's example is:

"Dear, dear friend, listen: if feeling like I am enough makes me become complacent, unmotivated, and full of myself, drastically compromising my relationship with others, then I don't want that either. And I appreciate you lookin' out. If I *have* to make a choice between feeling confident or pushing myself to give it my all and be kind and present with others, then I choose the latter. I promise. I promise to choose feeling really confident in myself and feeling good enough *only if it means I also stay authentic and humble*. Cool? We can have a *look* then? I hear you, and I really appreciate you looking out for me..."

You are making a promise with your subconscious to be in alignment with the highest intentions of your Soul—not your ego. If you consciously make this agreement by understanding the **wisdom that the limitation helped to build in your character**, your subconscious can now give you the go-ahead and release the chains so that you may rise and embody your next level. Getting your powerhouse on board and working on your behalf 24/7 creates life-changing effects.

Summary: Make a promise to your subconscious that you will be true to your highest core values.

Step 4: Find Exemplary Examples

Give yourself positive examples of whom in your life and/or in the world at large embodies genuine confidence, self-love, and feels good enough, while simultaneously upholding similar, moral values that you want to continue to embody.

For example: Think of people who are confident in themselves and have embodied their worth, but still continue to work hard, not get lazy, and continuously push themselves to the next level, while staying humble and heartfelt with others. Your subconscious will do anything you show it that it is possible. So come up with a solid list of examples to prove to yourself and your subconscious that your new strategy is absolutely possible.

Examples: Friends? Family?...Nelson Mandela, Oprah, Ellen DeGeneres, Richard Branson, etc.

Summary: Find inspiring examples of individuals who are embodying the qualities you desire.

Step 5: Solidify and Affirm

Anchor and remind yourself of your new perspective and truth. **The more committed you are to your new truth (rather than being one foot in and one foot out), the more you give your subconscious congruent, clear, consistent messages and the more it can execute powerfully on your behalf.**

Come up with an affirmation to remind yourself of your core desires, or as Collautt shares, "Your affirmation—you want to think of it as a sacred reminder of what is possible and reminds you of the ONLY road you can take in light of the promise you have made." Remind yourself by reading or saying your statement as often as feels good to you, and if possible, upon going to bed and rising, and/or after meditation as these are excellent times to access your subconscious mind.

For example: "Being good enough increases what I want in life. Being enough and loving myself allows me to fully embrace each day of my life. Being enough, loving myself, and being on my own side gives me courage and certainty to take action on what I want in life. I don't hold back because life is precious and I want to live my life to the fullest. I am strong; I am capable; I can overcome anything that comes my way. I am here to share my heart and gifts with the world, and if I ever fail, it will only be temporary. I choose to learn from any mistakes big or small, learning from them and *failing up*! I love myself and know that any rejection I encounter will help me grow stronger and wiser and keep me on the path of my destiny. I deeply love and value myself. I live courageously."

This was an example. Now write one for yourself and read it several times a day.

Summary: Write a sacred reminder that you read every day as it feels good to do so.

Step 6: Trust and Allow

You don't have to work for every detail yourself. Allow, believe, and trust that grace can and will happen in your life and beautiful changes and growth can occur in harmony by working with an intelligence greater than yourself—an intelligence that equally wants the very best for you. Life equally wants you to succeed!

Summary: Surrender, allow, and trust.

If you want to change and upgrade an unhealthy, anxiety-inducing, limiting belief, this exercise can be life changing and it takes as little to 30-60 minutes. Invest in the time to do this and get your powerhouse on board with what you consciously want—because what you tell yourself is everything. What you believe is possible for yourself is everything. You can't let the outside world or others define you—*you define yourself.* I hope the power of this sinks in, anchors in your knowing, and gives you clarity on why it is of the utmost importance to take the time to upgrade your beliefs to ones that support your highest expression.

To give your subconscious a powerful example of the life-changing power of beliefs, here is a transcript from a talk Oprah gave on her show, *Life Class*:

*"I grew up in rural Mississippi. A black girl. And at the time, we were called colored people. My grandmother was a maid—that was all she ever knew. And the only **real** expectation she held for me is that one day I would become a maid, and in her words, 'Have some good white folks.' Meaning people who would not speak negatively about me, who would allow me to take food home, who would be good to me, and treat me with some level of dignity and respect. That was my grandmother's dream for me, but I had another dream for myself—more than a dream, I had a **belief** for myself. And I remember watching her hang up clothes on the line and her saying, 'You better watch me Oprah Gail because one day you'll have to do this for yourself...' and **knowing** inside myself that that was **not** going to be my life. I don't know **how** I knew it, other than that thing that we all have— intuition or instinct that said, 'No, this will not be my life.'*

*"Because I **sensed that** and was **connected** to that—I remember it was a very still moment, and I was quiet and I was watching her—I can see it right now—she was putting clothes pins on the line and I could see her breath because it was cold, and I could see the moisture coming from her lips. And I **knew** that that would not be my life, I **knew** I would not be hanging clothes on a line in a backyard in Mississippi. I was either four or five years old. That **belief** that that would **not** be my life is what I held onto for the longest of times. No matter what, I **believed** that there was something bigger,*

*greater, and more for me. I had no idea that it would take the form that it has taken, that I would become a person on television, and that I would do all the things that I have done—because obviously when I was growing up there was no one like me on television, but I just **believed** that there was something **more**, and I was always cognizant of what that more was…There is a wonderful Bible passage that says, 'Be still and know that I am God.' You can't allow the voices of the world to drown out that which you know is the voice of God, the voice that is your own consciousness, the voice that is the purest light of yourself—for that is how the energy of God speaks to all of us. So know that number one—know that you are worthy and deserving of the **best** that Creation has to offer, and **believe** that there is a reason **why** you are here, and understand that it is **your** job is to figure out what that **is** and follow that belief."*

What you think about is what you bring about. Think about what you want, not what you don't want. Be a watch-guard of your thoughts. For as a small black girl who grew up in rural Mississippi, whose parents divorced when she was young, who was sexually abused growing up, and who overcame many more obstacles to become one of the world's most influential women and self-made billionaires…when she shares…

> **"What you believe has more power than what you dream or wish or hope for.**
> **You become what you believe."**

… I really hope you let these words sink in.

11

Bringing it All Together

To make it crystal clear how to bring everything we have covered together to self-heal your anxiety, I want to briefly summarize each piece of the Integrative Health process, so you can clearly see the path you can now choose to take.

A Simple Summary

Anxiety is a biological, purposeful, and intelligent response from your body giving you the energy and mental alertness you require to overcome a threat. Chronic symptoms are your body's form of communication, telling you that it is stuck in a perpetual state of tension due to unresolved stress affecting your mental, emotional, spiritual, and physical well-being. Furthermore, your unresolved stress often has a lineage of repeating, challenging themes that originated in childhood and strengthened overtime throughout your life; these unconscious patterns formed Achilles Heel triggers that make you overreact to life in anxious ways, coupled by a physiological stress response. Left unresolved, your unconscious stress patterns keep you chained to your past and stuck in a repeating pattern that accumulates more stress in your life, causing your symptoms to worsen overtime, while limiting your true expression, and negatively impacting the quality of your life.

The Good News

Your body is not separate from your thoughts and emotions— your body is your mirror. It is one of your greatest teachers *because it cannot lie*; therefore, through honoring your body and decoding its anxiety symptoms, you can know exactly what stress requires your attention. You have the opportunity to change your life and evolve *through* your greatest challenges by discovering how they have served you on the highest level. Instead of covering up your anxiety, you get to the heart of the matter and treat the core stress patterns; and in addressing the key problem, you take your power back from your deepest wounds by learning how the very thing that has caused you the most suffering in your life is actually connected to the very thing you love and value most. Through this process, you gain greater clarity and vision into who you are, and you can consciously start using your stress in a positive, healthy, life-changing way.

The Law of Conservation says that energy cannot be destroyed, it can only change form. When you transform anxious, wounded, static, emotional energy into love, meaning, and wisdom, the old energy transforms into its higher potential state of purpose and power. The self-healing journey not only resolves your anxiety from the inside out, but it wakes you up to who you really are, and what you would love to do with your life...and then gets you on the path of doing it.

Integrative Health Steps to Resolve Your Anxiety

Note: I suggest working with a trained professional on your core anxiety themes. I wrote this book primarily to empower you with new, invaluable information to help you resolve your anxiety from the inside out using an Integrative Health process. If you feel confident that you can clear your stress connected to your anxiety on your own, you can follow the steps below; however, if you have experienced traumas that are still especially upsetting to you, then it would be best for you to work with a trained professional. Trying to use self-healing techniques on your own without fully completing the process properly can make you feel more agitated if your stress is not 100% cleared. Please use your best judgment and know your limits.

First Step

You want to investigate the origins of your symptoms. Investigate what past stresses, and/or highly emotional, unexpected events might be connected to:

<u>Pharyngeal Arches</u>: Frontal Fear

Investigate your current life when you feel anxious about a future stress. For example, when do you experience being anxious or afraid that something bad is going to happen; are you worried that someone will be upset with you, criticize you, or get angry with you if you make a mistake?

With curiosity, now investigate this feeling back to its origin and ask yourself:

When was the first time I felt this feeling?

Is this feeling connected to when my parents were divorcing, when we moved unexpectedly, when I was being bullied, when I was criticized, when I was around an addicted parent, when there was fighting?

Thyroid Excretory Ducts: Powerlessness

Investigate in your current life when you experience anxiety and a feeling of powerlessness in your life. Does your anxiety get triggered when you feel like you are not in control and you feel ineffectual, helpless, and/or weak?

With curiosity, now investigate this feeling back to its origin and ask yourself:

When was the first time I felt this feeling?

Is this anxious, powerless feeling connected to when I saw my parents upset, and I couldn't do anything to make them feel better? Is it connected to when I moved towns or schools and didn't know how to make new friends? Did I feel anxious growing up when a lot of stress was happening around me and there was nothing I could do to stop it, make it better, or get away from it? Did I feel anxious and worried wishing I could solve a problem in my family, but ultimately, I didn't know what to do even though I felt it was my responsibility to solve the problem? Did I get yelled at or bullied and felt I was powerless to stop what was happening? Did I get abused mentally, emotionally, physically, or sexually and felt powerless to stop it?

Adrenal Medulla: Intolerable Stress

If you experience times of a significant drop in your energy levels and/or depression, you can look for stress related to the Adrenal Medulla. Again, be wise. If looking into your past is triggering you, be mindful of going deep into these memories without a qualified coach or therapist to support you.

Investigate your current life when you experience anxiety because you feel overwhelmed with unbearable or intolerable stress. Does your anxiety get triggered when you feel like you can't bear it anymore, when you feel you are at the end of your rope, when life is too much to handle, and/or when you are at your wits' end?

With curiosity and emotional calmness, now investigate this feeling back to its origin and ask yourself:

When was the first time I felt this feeling?

Is this anxious feeling of overwhelm connected to when I saw my parents fighting or when they got a divorce? Is this feeling of being worried from when I couldn't manage everything that was happening when my parents couldn't afford to pay rent or buy us food for the week? Is it connected to when my parent or a loved one died and it was too much for me to handle and cope with—and I was terrified and anxious about the unknown, followed by feelings of 'it is too much, what is the point, life is too hard, what does it matter?' Did I ever feel this when someone broke up with me unexpectedly and I didn't know how to cope with all my emotions?

Second Step

Once you find the Frontal Fear, Powerlessness theme and possibly the Intolerable Stress, you'll want to investigate further to uncover the track patterns and repeating themes. In chronological order, write down a list of significant memories when you experienced Frontal Fear, Powerlessness, and perhaps Intolerable Stress. (The same as you did with the rejection and failure exercise.)

Third Step

Make your unconscious conscious. What is your limiting belief about these reoccurring anxiety inducing themes? Underneath the events, what beliefs did you make about yourself, life, and/or others?

Fourth Step

Resolve your stress using a transformational self-healing modality.

- You can work with a trained META-Health Coach, a Demartini Method Facilitator, or me in my intensive programs.
- Visit my website if you would like to schedule a consultation, if you would like learn about my online class teaching the Demartini Method @ www.belladodds.com, or for referrals.

There are many powerful self-healing modalities that you can use. I have shared with you the Demartini Method because it is a profound and highly effect technique for even the most challenging past experiences. I also see that it greatly helps individuals awaken to their life's purpose, empowering them with confidence, certainty, and vitality—all of which are healthy mental and emotional states of consciousness for your body. However, the Demartini Method is not the only technique available.

Other techniques I highly recommend:

- *EFT* – Emotional Freedom Technique
- *Faster EFT* – *(This can be a very powerful clean up/self-healing tool)*
- *Timeline Therapy with NLP* – Neuro-Linguistic Programming
- *EMDR* – Eye Movement Desensitization and Reprocessing
- *ACE* – Advanced Clearing Energetics

Additionally, there are techniques to support your equilibrium and combat the constant, daily barrage of 21st century stress:

- Meditation
- I have a free anxiety-calming guided meditation you can download from my website at www.belladodds.com
- *TM* – *Transcendental Meditation* (I was trained in this and find it to be a powerful technique; however, it is expensive and can cost up to $2,000 to learn in the United States.)
- *Primordial Sound Meditation* – Deepak and Oprah have several meditations you can buy online, and they release several new meditations during the year that you can try out for free. These meditations, like TM, have a mantra, which assist your mind to elevate to a higher state of consciousness, calming and healing your

nervous system, and filling your *being* with peace, oneness, and serenity. I find Deepak's meditation to be just as powerful as Transcendental Meditation, and the cost is much more affordable at around $40.00 for 20 different mantras.

- Yoga – All forms from rigorous to restorative.
- Kundalini Yoga
- Quick emergency fix is to put an ice pack on your forehead and back of your neck. You can also put a hot pack on your lower back if you have one. Lie down for 10 minutes and focus on slowing your breath, lengthening your exhalation, and bringing your energy out of your head and into your lower body. The opposite temperatures of hot and cold on your spine help to relax your cranial sacral and central nervous system. It feels really good and is very relaxing. Give it a try! You can also do this while listening to my meditation or other calming music.
- Learn a mindfulness practice. You can work with a practitioner, read a book, or take a class on mindfulness.
- Seek to get a good restful night sleep.
- Consistently eat a healthy, balanced diet.
- Notice when you are being overly critical of yourself—stop—literally turn down the volume in your head.
- Minimize refined sugar, caffeine, and alcohol.
- Workout/exercise in balanced moderation. Don't overstress your body with extreme workouts that have been shown to cause insomnia, mood swings, adrenal fatigue, hormonal changes (women losing their menstrual cycle), etc.
- Be mindful of not being on a low-carb restrictive diet *and* exercising in excess. In your attempts to be overly

healthy, you may be doing harm to your body. I have worked with many clients who burned their bodies out and had various health problems of chronic fatigue, digestive issues, brain fog/inability to focus, loss of sex drive, depression, etc. by trying to be the new modern version of sexy—zero body fat and a perfectly sculpted physique that they made themselves very ill and compromised their metabolism. A lower metabolism can cause a cooler body temperature, and from here, many health problems can arise. If this sounds like something you are struggling with, I recommend reading Matt Stone's *Diet Recovery 2* or *Eat for Heat.*

Fifth Step

Upgrade unhealthy, stress-inducing, limiting beliefs. After resolving your stress using a transformational self-healing technique and changing your story, you are now ready to upgrade your beliefs. There are many ways you can do this. In the previous chapter, I provided you with just one example from Dr. Collautt. You can also try using:

- EFT
- Faster EFT
- NLP
- The Work by Byron Katie
- Access Consciousness

Anxiety, fearful beliefs of *I am not safe, I am going to get in trouble,* or *something bad is going to happen* are all intense fears to upgrade—but you absolutely can! You need to:

1. Have a deep desire to upgrade a limiting belief to an empowering one.

2. Logically see how this belief got created and how it is limiting your power, life, and health.
3. Decide that you want to upgrade your story to an empowered, adult, wise perspective.
4. Create space from the intensity of a belief.
5. Allow yourself to stop being identified with a 'lie' that is holding you back and is unhealthy for you.
6. Realize that only you have the ability to change your belief—no one else can do it for you.
7. Be excited to change it! Upgrade your belief with certainty and commitment. Use the exercise in this book to upgrade your belief by using the power of your subconscious mind.
8. Create an affirmation to remind yourself of your new truth: I am safe. Everything is going to be okay. Everything is going to work out for my highest good.
9. Consciously work to retrain your physiology, thoughts, and perceptions by telling your body it is okay and that you are safe. Remind yourself as often as necessary to help you operate from an empowered adult perspective, not from a disempowered seven-year-old, fearful child's perspective.
10. In addition to safe and secure beliefs, write inspiring and uplifting beliefs.
11. Place your hands on your heart and say: I am made of love. I am made of love. I am made of love…and then add on new beliefs you would love to anchor in your life.
12. Remember that persistence pays. Persistence and patience are the name of this game! Keep going. Don't give up and don't lose faith. Undoing decades of stressful patterns is a process, so walk the journey, day by day, baby steps make your way steadily up the mountain. Remember your commitment and belief in

your Self is your most powerful medicine. You are worthy of your beautiful light. Don't ever give up on yourself and you will succeed.

Your beliefs become your thoughts
Your thoughts become your words
Your words become your actions
Your actions become your habits
Your habits become your values
Your values become your destiny

~ Gandhi

Sixth Step

Believe in yourself and own your worth. HONOR the gifts you have been given and give them back to the world. Believe in yourself and your Soul's Purpose.

Seventh Step

Don't listen to voices that are unhealthy. Be mindful with whom you share the wisdom and insights you've attained along your self-healing journey. Attune to your inner truth and knowing. Trust yourself.

Eighth Step

Keep learning. Read books that have helped other individuals change their lives and do amazing things. Give yourself healthy role models to inspire you. Fill your mind with empowered and wise teachings. *Think and Grow Rich*, the original unabridged edition was written by Napoleon Hill in 1937 and is a gem to learn about the power of your mind to influence your life and destiny.

Ninth Step

Enjoy the adventure of your self-healing journey. It has the opportunity to be one of the most sacred, intimate, and transformative journeys you will ever take. Honor your Soul's essence and know that life is conspiring in your favor, in miraculous ways, to help you succeed.

And remember you are powerful.

Believe in your ability to overcome your greatest challenges...and you will most certainly find a way to make it so.

In Closing

It is an inspiration to be able to contribute to the exciting, global movement taking place within health and healing during the 21st century and to have this opportunity to share invaluable, life-changing information with you. For thousands of years, each century has built upon the next, furthering our progress and understanding of health, healing, science, consciousness, and spirituality. This book shares within it an evolutionary understanding of wisdom and knowledge built upon the ages, and if it were not for the countless individuals who dedicated their lives to advance our understanding of science and healing, this book could not have been written. I am forever grateful to all the Souls who have contributed to humanity in progressing our understanding of human health, past and present. I thank you with all of my heart! In addition, many of the insights shared within *The Anxiety Solution* are due to the amazing individuals I have been blessed to work with, who have courageously allowed me to walk side by side with them on their most sacred, self-healing journeys. You know who you are and please know this book would not have been possible without you!

I thank you for coming along with me on this journey. I hope this book has given you new, invaluable information that you can use to resolve your anxiety from the inside out and change your life for the better. I do not believe that the sun, moon, trees, oceans, and miracles of life on Earth were all created so that you might just cope...and not *really live.* I believe the blessings of all of these marvels were created for you to be able to add your unique genius and beautiful light expression into this world in the way that *only you can.* I believe whole-heartedly that the world needs you to rise up and be your fullest expression; to share your gifts, and to help solve problems that you would love to bring your genius to. Whether your inspired purpose is to be a parent, an artist, a business owner, a teacher, an architect, a philanthropist, it matters not—as long as it is deeply meaningful to you and calls forth the very best in you.

Know that I am sending you courage, strength, and love!

~ May you rise to meet your journey ~

In Love and Light,

Bella xo

A Gift for You

I could have written another book to cover everything you need to know about anxiety and resolving your symptoms! If you liked what you have read and would like to learn more of what I have to share, you can sign up for my newsletter to receive emails of the most recent breakthroughs in integrative health, as well as hear interviews from leading experts in the field of healing and science. My site was created to be an ongoing educational resource to offer you the latest breakthroughs in health and healing methodologies. As a bonus, you can also download your free gift—a twelve minute calming and guided meditation to soothe your anxious mind and relax your nervous system. To sign up for the newsletter or download your free gift, please go to: www.belladodds.com/meditation.

One Small Favor

As you know, Integrative Health is a revolution taking place as millions around the world are changing the status quo of how we look at and treat disease. If you found *The Anxiety Solution* helpful to you and believe others would greatly benefit from it, I would be grateful if you would take a few minutes to share your thoughts on Amazon. Your experience could help others, as well as support the evolutionary leap in how we honor a human being on all levels when treating health problems and disease.

I thank you for letting me support you on your self-healing journey. Sharing this work with you is truly an honor.

About the Author

Bella Dodds is the author of *The Anxiety Solution* and *The Butterfly Story*. As an Integrative Health coach with fourteen years experience in the healing arts, Bella specializes in anxiety, specifically educating clients on how their mental and emotional stress can lead to physical symptoms in their body. To solve this problem, Bella has developed an integrative health process that is both deeply rewarding and life-changing, while simultaneously supporting individuals to resolve their symptoms from the inside out. To that end, she founded the website Belladodds.com as an ongoing educational resource to share breakthroughs in health, healing, and scientific discoveries for those seeking to expand their knowledge and understand the power they possess to impact their own health. Bella's work is far-reaching as her coaching practice, workshops, and ongoing webinars extend this self-healing process with individuals from around the world. Bella is also personally committed to supporting and finding solutions to clean energy technology, to eliminate child sex slavery, to empower women entrepreneurs in 3rd world countries, and to preserve threatened forests and pristine habitats in the environment. A percentage of proceeds from both publications and her practice will be directed toward funding solutions to these global problems.

Made in the USA
Middletown, DE
30 March 2015

SECTION THREE